Special Thanks To,

Anna Doudenina for helping me to turn my idea of this book to a reality

The Self-Taught Software Tester

A Step By Step Guide to Learn
Software Testing Using Real-Life Project

Chhavi Raj Dosaj

The Self-Taught Software Tester
A Step By Step Guide to Learn Software Testing Using Real-Life Project

By Chhavi Raj Dosaj

Contents

About the book

To successfully perform the job of the software tester/ test analyst you should have a sound knowledge of testing fundamentals and should be able to correlate that knowledge with the experience you have learned while working as a tester on a software project. This book will teach you both, the first half of the book provides a detailed explanation of the fundamentals of software testing and the second half focuses on a step by step walk-through of a real-life testing project. This will help you to understand how the real software projects are run from start to end and where the testing fits in the big picture of the project lifecycle. The book provides details of each testing activities which will help you to understand how the test activities are planned, executed and monitored in real projects. This book is a roadmap, a guide to understanding the bits and pieces of software testing and how you can apply them when you are working as a tester on a project. This book will teach you each and everything you should know about software testing with references to a real-life project. This book will not only help you in securing your first testing job but will also guide you on your day-to-day journey as a software tester.

This book is divided into two parts -the first part talks about the need for software testing, different type and levels of testing and how they are performed at each project level. The second part uses a real-life testing project to give you more contexts around these software testing fundamentals. The book will traverse the journey of the software tester working through different testing activities in the projects with minute details. User Interface (UI) of the system is provided so you can get a visual impression of the look and feel of the system. The templates of project documents will help you to understand the entire test management process.

Some of the chapters are not necessarily meant for the software testers as they are not directly involved in those activities but knowing them will help you to understand the big picture and will keep you ready for your first testing job.

If you are new to testing, you may find some of the topics too technical. My advice is to skim through these topics and move forward. Once you have finished the entire book you can revisit them, by the time these topics will be easier to understand.

Acknowledgments

I would like to thanks my colleagues from the **Reserve Bank of Australia** for helping me with the book.

Sandeep Jain- Solution Architect for the solution design diagrams,

Hari Yagnamurthy- Senior Business Analyst for helping me with the business requirements,

Anna Douderina- UI designer for creating the wireframes for the IMT project web pages,

Arun Sree Kumar for creating the diagrams for the book.

Disclaimer

1   What is Software Testing

This section explores what is software testing and why is it necessary?

Testing helps in finding the defects in the software before they cause failures in the live environment

On June 4, 1996, an unmanned Ariane 5 rocket was launched by the European space agency. The rocket failed after 37½ seconds of its lift-off from French Guiana. The rocket was on its first voyage, after a decade of development costing $7 billion. The destroyed rocket and its cargo were valued at $500 million. A board of inquiry investigated the causes of the explosion and in two weeks issued a report. It turned out that the cause of the failure was a software error in the inertial reference system. This software error resulted in a rocket to deviate from its vertical ascent, and the self-destruct capabilities were enacted before the unpredictable flight path resulted in a bigger problem. This scenario was not considered and tested during the formal testing of the software used in the rocket otherwise it would have been caught and rectified earlier.

The main purpose of testing is to find defects before they become failures in the real environment (production environment). Therefore, tests are designed in such a way that they can find as many defects as possible before the system goes live.

Testing ensures that the system meets the user requirements

One of the government motor registry agencies decided to implement new vehicle registration software. The new software was designed to replace all the manual processes involved in issuing a driver licence resulting in fast turnaround time for the customer. The contract for building this new software was given to a major software development company. During the initial phase, the agency worked closely with the development company to specify the requirements for this new system. But during the testing, it was found that the system is not capable to handle many of the functions which were specified initially. The reason was that the software developers were not able to understand the requirements properly and have not coded those functions correctly.

One of the other important purposes of testing is to make sure that the user requirements are fulfilled in the system, otherwise, the software will not perform as intended. When the project is started the user-requirements are captured which becomes the basis for the specifications such as Business Requirements Document (BRD). These specification documents are used as the basis for creating test cases for testing. These test cases are run later to make sure that all the business requirements are covered by testing. **Traceability is created between test cases and requirements** to make sure that test cases have covered all the requirements. This way the testing can assure that the software will work according to the user requirements when it is used by the real users.

Testing helps to minimize the risk

One of the software development company is involved in the development of an automatic flight control system and a video game system. The testing performed for both systems will not be the same as the risk of failure is greater for a flight control system as compared to the video game system.

Risk is inherent in all software development. If the system fails it may cause loss of time, loss of money or even injury or death based on where the software is used. These uncertainties become more significant as the system complexity and the implications of failure increase. Intuitively, there is a greater probability of failure in the more complex system and the impact of the failure is also greater. What we test, and how much we test, is directly related in some way to the risk. Greater risk implies rigorous and more testing.

Product risk means that the product or software build will not meet the purpose for which it is being built. This might be because the original design was flawed, or the features had not been properly coded. A common example is failure-prone software delivered or a defect in the software which could cause harm to an individual or company.

During the initial phase of project initiation, product risks are identified, test cases are then created to cover these identified risks and the appropriate testing is done to make sure that the risk is minimized to an acceptable level (more rigorous testing for the high-risk item and less for low-risk items).

Testing reduces the product risk as most of the defects related to the system are uncovered by testing during the testing phase, so there are less chances of system failing when it is used by the customers or users in the live environment.

Testing finds the Quality Level of the software and helps in decision making

In early Jan 2018, Apple announced that some features planned for its iPhone operating system (iOS 12) may be delayed for a year. During the testing, many quality issues in the iOS software were found. Apple took this information seriously as it is one of the companies which lays great emphasis on software quality and delayed the release of these features.

In the projects, often the project stakeholders are interested to know about the level of quality before they are comfortable releasing the software to the customer. The results from testing provide them this information. One of the key indicators for the **level of quality is based on the number of defects found** during testing and the **outstanding defects** which still need to be fixed.

The quality is also the amount of fulfillment of expectations. On the one hand, we have some expectations(requirements), and on the other hand, we have the product that should fulfill these expectations. The test helps to find out how close is the product in fulfilling these expectations. This information helps the stakeholders in decision making.

Testing ensures that the system is fit for the purpose it is built

A major Australian Bank upgraded its banking system so the Tax and Financial files of business customers can be uploaded directly to the system. During the initial testing, testers tried uploading files in different formats to make sure the system is working properly. The system could upload these files without any problem and the team was convinced that this functionality is working properly. Later during the business testing, the system crashed when the business users tried to test the system with the replica of real tax and financial files. The reason was that the real tax and financial files were generally more than 10 MB size but during the earlier testing testers used small size files which were few KBs so the problem could not be found earlier.

Often the initial testing is done to find the defects but having no defects doesn't mean that the system is fit for the purpose. Before the software is released to the live environment a level of **user testing is done to make sure that the system is fit for the purpose**, this also helps to build user confidence in the system.

There are different phases of testing each having different objectives. The objective of the user acceptance testing phase which is performed after all the other testing phases is to find out whether the software is fit for the purpose. We will discuss these different phases or levels of testing with their objectives later in the book.

Testing simulates the real-time scenarios

On July 1, 2012, the Australian government introduced a new online system for immigration. As the system was designed to handle the applications on the first come first serve basis, all the applicants rushed to apply on 1st Jul morning. They were able to access the system but when many people tried to submit their application the system crashed. The performance of the website proved inadequate under this load and the website had to be taken offline. Running a test through a software system can only show that one or more defects exist. **Testing cannot show that the software is**

error-free. The system was functionally working fine but the non-functional testing was not done properly to cater to this load, therefore, this performance peaks beyond the capacity of the website caused the system to be unavailable for many hours.

Performance tests are run during testing to mimic the real-time scenario for example, how many multiple users can login or do a particular operation simultaneously. This can help in identifying the performance-related issues of the system under load.

From the above examples, we can infer that software testing is a way to **assess the quality of the software** and to **reduce the risk of software failure** in operation.

The above scenarios also explain that if the software is tested properly then we can avoid failures when the system is live, but it is seldom the case.

One of the reasons is that testing everything is not possible. For most of the systems, exhaustive testing is not possible, that is we can't exercise all the combinations of input and preconditions. Let us use a simple example to understand exhaustive testing. The software under test is having a one-digit field that accepts only upper-case alphabet character. If we use exhaustive testing techniques, the valid inputs are 26 uppercase alphabet characters. Consider using the exhaustive testing technique on a one-digit field of software that accepts only upper-case alphabets. In this case, valid tests are required to check all 26 uppercase alphabets are accepted. We need to test that all invalid inputs are also rejected. Tests will be required for 0-9 digits, 26 lower case alphabet characters, and 32 special characters including space. Therefore a total of 94 test cases is required to fully test this one-digit field. If we try the exhaustive testing technique for software having 10 input fields where each input can have 5 possible values. Then just to test all the valid input value combination would be 10 to power 5 (10^5) which is 10x10x10x10x10=100,000 test cases, it is unlikely that these many test cases can be tested.

Even for these small systems, there are many, many possible data combinations to attempt. It is not possible to say whether there are any outstanding defects until all possible input combinations have been tried and it is not possible to test all possible combinations of data input and circumstances.

For this reason, **risk and priorities are used to concentrate on the most important aspects to test**. Both 'risk' and 'priorities' are covered later in more detail. Their use is important to ensure that the most important functions of the system are tested first.

Testing is also context-dependent. This means that different type of testing is necessary for different circumstances. A website where information can merely be viewed will be tested in a different way to an e-commerce site, where goods can be bought using credit cards. We need to test an air traffic control system with more rigor than a system for social networking. Risk can be a large factor in determining the type of testing that is needed. The higher the possibility of losses, the more we need to invest in testing the software before it is implemented.

2 Software Development Models

To have a better understanding of testing, it is important to be familiar with the software development lifecycle first and then see how the different testing activities fit in this lifecycle. A software development lifecycle model describes the types of activity performed at each stage in a software development project, and how the activities relate to one another logically and chronologically. There are a number of different software development lifecycle models, each of which requires different approaches to testing.

Common software development lifecycle falls into one of the following categories:

- Sequential development models
- Iterative and incremental development models

Sequential development model

A sequential development model describes the software development process as a linear, sequential flow of activities. This means that any phase in the development process should only begin when the previous phase is complete. In theory, there is no overlap of phases, but in most of the projects, there is a slight overlap of phases. This enables some early feedback from the following phase.

Examples of sequential development model are:

- Waterfall model
- V-model

Waterfall Model

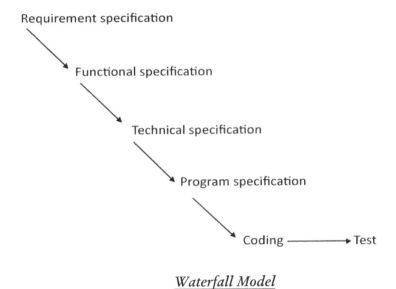

Waterfall Model

In the Waterfall model, there is a separate phase for each development activity. The typical phases in the waterfall model are requirements analysis, design, coding, and testing.

These phases are completed one after another. In this model, test activities only occur after all other development activities have been completed.

V- Model

V-model is the extension of the waterfall model. The V-model integrates the test process throughout the development process to implement the principle of early testing.

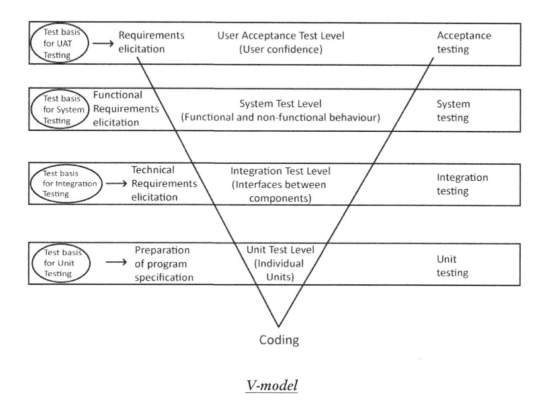

V-model

The V-model includes test levels associated with each corresponding development phase; A common type of V-model is shown above.

The activities on the left-hand side of the V-model focuses on work-product creation for elaborating the initial requirements and then providing more technical detail for the development:

- **Requirement specification**—capturing of user needs.
- **Functional specification**—definition of functions required to meet user needs.
- **Technical specification**—technical design or architecture of functions identified in the functional specification.
- **Program specification**—detailed design of each module or unit to be built to meet the required functionality.

There is a relationship between the work products on the left-hand side and the testing activities on the right-hand side. Each work product can be **verified** by using static testing techniques (e.g. reviews) ensuring that the requirements as stated have been met. **Verification** helps to ensure that we are building the product in the right way.

The middle of the V-model shows that planning for testing can start as soon as the work-products for a particular development phase are ready. For example, once the requirement specifications are ready, planning for acceptance testing can be started.

The right-hand side focuses on the testing activities (**dynamic testing**).

- Testing against the program specification takes place at the unit testing stage.
- Testing against the technical specification takes place at the integration testing stage
- Testing against the functional specification takes place at the system testing stage.
- Testing against the requirement specification takes place at the acceptance testing stage.

The right-hand side of the V- model **validates** the requirement using the dynamic testing techniques. **Validation** ensures that requirements, as stated, have been met.

Iterative and incremental development models

Iterative development is the process of establishing requirements, designing, building and testing a system, done as a series of smaller incremental developments. In iterative development, the requirements can be clarified or discovered as the number of iterations increases. The approach is to 'build a little, test a little'. Each iteration provides feedback for the next iteration. Once each iteration has been completed the testing of the new elements of software must be tested with the existing unchanged software, thus it is necessary to perform regression testing after every single iteration.

Iterative & incremental development

Examples are:

Rational Unified Process: Each iteration tends to be relatively long (e.g., two to three months), and the feature increments are correspondingly large, such as two or three groups of related features

Scrum (Agile): Each iteration tends to be relatively short (e.g., days or weeks), and the feature increments are correspondingly small, such as a few enhancements and/ or two or three new features

Kanban (Agile): Implemented with or without fixed-length iterations, which can deliver either a single enhancement or feature upon completion, or can group features together to release at once

Spiral: Involves creating experimental increments. Some of these increments may be re-worked or even discarded in subsequent development work

The increment produced by an iteration may be tested at several levels as part of its development. An increment added to previously developed & tested functionality, forms a growing partial system, which should also be tested.

Regression testing is increasingly important on all iterations after the first one. Verification and validation can be carried out on each increment.

Incremental development involves establishing requirements, designing, building, and testing a system in pieces, which means that the software's features grow incrementally. The size of these feature increments varies, with some methods having larger pieces and some smaller pieces. The feature increments can be as small as a single change to a user interface screen or new query option.

3 | Types of Testing

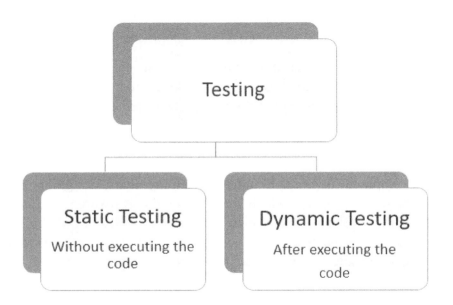

Static and Dynamic Testing

At a high level, there are two classification of testing- static and dynamic testing. The testing which is done after the execution of the code of a system being tested is called **dynamic testing**. The testing which can be done without the execution of the code of a system being tested is called **static testing**.

Static testing can be performed even before the coding of the software is started. Static testing finds and prevents defects by reviewing work products such as requirements, design documents, and source code. This makes corrections easier and cheaper to fix rather than finding the same defects late during the test execution. Static testing is done using **reviews** which involve manual examination of the project work products.

Following reviews could be applied in the projects:

• *Informal review (e.g., buddy check, pairing, pair review)*

Informal reviews have **no formal process defined** and may be as simple as a tester reviewing a buddy's test cases, or a team leader reviewing the output of one of their team members. Documentation of the review is not mandated but is sometimes produced.

The main purpose of an informal review is to find defects. It usually requires little investment, due to the lack of any formal process being required, but can be effective, depending on the skills and motivation of the reviewer.

• *Walkthrough*

Walkthroughs are typically used to check early drafts of work products. For instance, in the case of a new design, a walkthrough can allow a peer group to gain a better understanding of the approach being taken in the design. In return, those in attendance can offer guidance on the process.

The main purposes can be to find defects and improve the software product and possible additional purposes can be training for participants and achieving consensus.

• *Technical review*

A technical review has a well-defined process, generating records of errors found and actions to be taken. The review meeting is conducted as a formal meeting, with a defined facilitator (who must not be the author). This person is ideally trained in conducting reviews.

Reviewers have technical expertise in their disciplines, relevant to the work product being reviewed.

Pre-meeting preparation is essential for a formal review and typically checklists are used, and a report prepared, though these aspects are not mandatory.

A technical review is usually conducted to do one or more of the following: discuss, make decisions, evaluate alternatives, find defects, solve technical problems or check conformance to specifications and standards.

• *Inspection*

Inspections are the most formal type of reviews and focus on a particular work product. They were introduced at IBM in the early 1970s by Michael Fagan and have been praised as one of the single most significant process changes.

Inspections require a trained moderator, who should not be the author and all inspector roles are defined before the inspection.

Inspections follow a formal process based on rules and checklists and the process includes entry and exit criteria. Metrics are collected and used to improve processes as well as documents.

Pre-meeting preparation is essential and an inspection report with a list of findings is a mandatory component, as is a formal follow-up process.

The main purpose of an inspection is to find defects, but the process can also be used for initiating process improvements based on the metrics that are gathered.

Dynamic testing can be performed only after the code is executed. Dynamic testing verifies the behavior of the software and checks whether it is working as per the specifications. It also helps to identify any run time errors which cannot be found during static testing. This testing can start as soon as the smallest piece of code that can be executed independently is ready. At different levels of code completion, the scope of testing will change. Dynamic testing can be divided into different test levels. Each test level represents a group of test activities that are organized and managed together. The different test levels for dynamic testing are:

- Component/Unit testing
- Component Integration testing
- System testing
- System Integration testing
- Acceptance testing

For each dynamic test level, a suitable test environment is required. For example, in component testing, the developers typically use a local development environment but for acceptance testing, a production-like test environment is ideal.

To get a better understanding of test levels we will use a sample application called E-SYSTEM. This application allows customers to check their electricity usage online.

There are three components/units in this application

Login – This is used to enable sign-in for the customers using their LoginID/ password

Usage – This is to display the customer's current meter reading

Logout – This is used to sign-out the customer from the application.

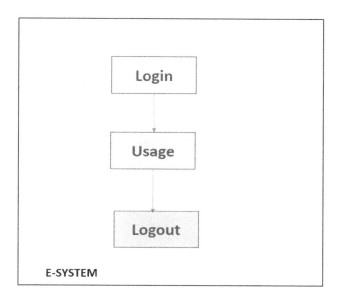

Component or unit testing

Component testing (also known as unit or module testing) focuses on separately testable components.

Component testing is often done in isolation from the rest of the component of the system, Component testing may cover functional characteristics (e.g., the correctness of calculations), non-functional characteristics (e.g., searching for memory leaks), and structural properties (e.g., checking the statement and decisions in the code).

If we refer our sample application E-SYSTEM, developers will develop Login, Usage and Logout components in isolation with other components. The testing for each module will also be done independently of each other.

Component testing is usually performed by the developer after the code is written for a component.

Note
• The purpose of **component testing** is to ensure that the code written for the component meets its specification, before its integration with other components.
• Performed by developers who have coded the component.
• Conducted in the development environment.
• Defects found are fixed as soon as they are found without going through a defect management process.

Component Integration testing

After the individual components are developed, they need to be integrated and tested. Unit Integration Testing is done after these individual units are combined and tested as a group. The purpose of this level of testing is to focus on the interactions between software components and expose faults in the interaction between integrated units.

Component integration testing is often the responsibility of developers and the testing is done in the development environment.

There are three commonly used integration strategies, as follows:

Big-Bang Integration

This is where all the components are integrated into one step resulting in a complete system.

If Big-Bang integration is used for our sample application all the modules

Login, Usage, and Logout should be ready and then linked at once.

Top-Down Integration

This is where the system is built in stages, starting with components that call other components. Components that call others are usually placed above those that are called. Top-down integration testing will permit the tester to evaluate component interfaces, starting with those at the 'top'.

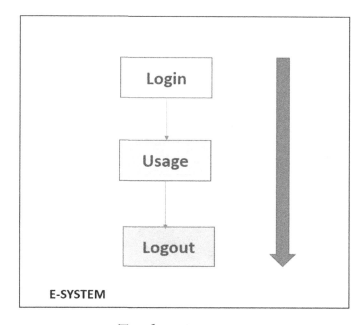

Top-down Integration

The control structure of a program can be represented in a diagram above. **Login** will call component **Usage**. The component **Usage** will be calling the **Logout** component. The integration order will be:

- Login, Usage
- Usage, Logout

In this case, while testing the first scenario, if the Usage component is not ready, a skeletal implementation of the component called stub will be created. **A stub is a passive component, called by other components**. In this case, this stub will just return two values "successful login" for right LoginID/ password combination and "unsuccessful login" for the wrong LoginID/password combination. These two values are sufficient to test the Login module.

Bottom-up Integration

This is the opposite of top-down integration and the components are integrated in bottom-up order.

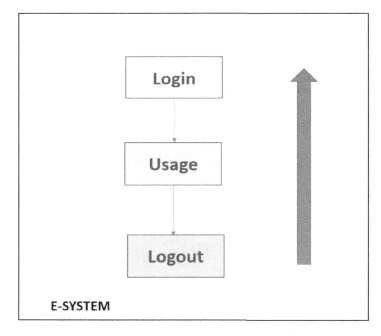

Bottom-up integration

The integration order will be:

- Logout, Usage,
- Usage, Login

In bottom-up integration when testing the first scenario if the **Usage** component is not built yet, then we have to use a component called **driver** to replace it. **Drivers are Active component which are calling other components.** They are generally more complex than stubs.

To simplify defect isolation and detect defects early, integration should normally be incremental rather than "big bang". A risk analysis of the most complex interfaces can help to focus on integration testing.

Note

A Stub is a skeletal or special-purpose implementation of a software component, used to develop or test a component that calls or is otherwise dependent on it. It replaces a "called" component.

A Driver is a software component or test tool that replaces a component that takes care of the control and/or the calling of a component or system.

Note

- The purpose of **component integration testing** is to expose defects in the interactions between integrated components and is done after component testing.
- Performed by the developers who have coded the components
- Conducted in the development environment

System testing (ST)

System testing focuses on the **behavior and capabilities of a whole system** or product, often considering the end-to-end tasks the system can perform and the non-functional behaviors it exhibits while performing those tasks.

The tests for system testing are created based on the business requirements which are often created by business analysts in the projects.

System testing often produces information that is used by stakeholders to make release decisions. System testing may also satisfy legal or regulatory requirements or standards.

System testing should focus on the overall, end-to-end behavior of the system as a whole. System testing should investigate both the **functional and non- functional** requirements of the system.

The testing team typically carries out system testing in the testing environment.

Note
• The purpose of **system testing** is to validate the behavior of the system as a whole
• Performed by the testing team

System Integration testing (SIT)

System integration testing focuses on the interactions between different systems and mostly done after system testing. System integration testing can also cover interactions with the interfaces provided by external organizations (e.g., web services). SIT tests expose any gaps in the system interaction with other applications.

While the ST test cases are focused on the Individual System under test, SIT test cases are focused on feeding the data to other systems or receiving the data from other systems.

The system integration testing is performed in the testing environment by the testing team. Testers performing system integration testing should understand the system architecture and should have influenced integration planning.

If our sample application E-SYSTEM is passing the USAGE data to an external application BILLING which processes this information to generate an invoice for the customer. To verify that the data is passed correctly to the BILLING application for processing will be the scope of system integration testing.

For system integration testing there is also a possibility that one of the external systems is not ready or not accessible for testing. In this case, **simulators** are used to mimic these external systems.

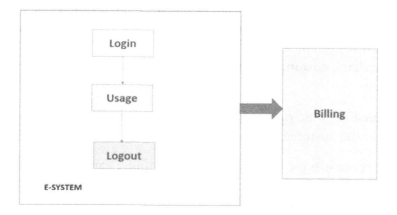

Note
• The purpose of **system integration testing** is to test interactions between different systems or between hardware and software.
• Performed by a tester who understands the overall architecture
• Conducted in a testing environment.
• A Simulator is a device, computer program, or system used during testing, which behaves or operates like a given system when provided with a set of controlled inputs.

Note

Let's take a simple example to have a better understanding of ST and SIT. The system under test is an Auto Finance system that is used by car dealers to finance the cars for their customers. This system has an interface that the dealers use to collect the personal and financial information of their customers. Once the details are submitted this system will feed this data to an external Credit Check System which will check the customer credit history and will send a score back to the Auto Finance system.

The scores came in three ranges from the Credit Check system. The decision to lend the loan to the customer can be made using the following rules:

- If the score is high, then the loan application is auto accepted.
- If the score is medium, then the lender must manually review and process the loan application.
- If the score is low the loan application is auto rejected.

ST test cases will be focused on testing the Auto finance system, doing field-level validation for dealer interface like customer name, date of birth, address, etc. ST testing will also check that all the customer information which is entered through the interface is processed correctly to the database.

SIT test cases will be focused around checking different credit scores from the Credit Check System based on different customer profiles. To perform SIT Credit Check testing environment of the system should be hooked up to the Auto Finance test environment and the test data (customer profiles) used for testing should be present in Credit Check system environment. Based on the customer profiles testers can verify all three scenarios as mentioned earlier. SIT testing will prove that the Credit System can process the input data correctly passed from the Auto finance system as well as the output(score) generated by the Credit System is passed and processed correctly by the Auto finance system.

User Acceptance Testing (UAT)

Acceptance testing of the system is typically focused on validating the fitness for use of the system by intended users in a real or simulated operational environment.

The main objective is to check whether the system is fit for purpose and building confidence that the users can use the system to meet their needs, fulfill requirements, and perform business processes with minimum difficulty, cost, and risk. Acceptance testing may also satisfy legal or regulatory requirements or standards.

Test cases for UAT testing are written based on the initial customer requirement, it should be performed by the customer or customer representatives (the business team who work closely with the customer).

UAT is performed in the UAT test environment (different from system testing environment) which is similar to the production environment, this helps in finding any defects or issues which occur only in a production-like environment.

Functional and Non-functional testing

Functional testing of a system involves tests that evaluate functions that the system should perform. It is the testing of **"what"** the system should do and can be unique to a system. For an airline website, user function can be search for a flight and book a flight. For ATM software, the user functions can be check balance, withdraw cash, change pin. Functional requirements may be described in work products such as requirements specification, use cases, functional specifications, etc.

Functional test design and execution may involve special skills or knowledge. It can be the knowledge of the particular business problem the software solves (e.g., payment software for the banking industry).

Examples include Regression Testing, System Testing, and System Integration Testing.

Non-functional testing evaluates software product quality characteristics of systems. These quality characteristics may relate to usability, reliability, portability, performance efficiency or security of the system.

These tend to be generic requirements, which can be applied to many different systems. They will cover questions such as:

- How many concurrent users can the system support?
- How long is the data held locally before it is archived?
- How long will it take for a webpage to download?
- How many transactions can occur in a period of time?
- What is the maximum number of transactions that can take place?

Non-functional testing is the testing of "**how well**" the system behaves. Examples include Performance (Load & Stress), Dependability, Robustness, Usability, Reliability, Portability, Interoperability, Maintainability, Resilience & Recoverability testing. Non-functional test design and execution may involve special skills or knowledge.

Note
Testing evaluates both functional and non-functional quality characteristics of the software.

Different Test techniques

The purpose of a test technique is to identify test conditions, test cases, and test data. It is a classic distinction to denote test techniques as black-box, white-box, or experience-based.

Black-box test techniques (also called behavioral or behavior-based techniques) are used to derive and select test conditions or test cases, based on the analysis of the test basis documentation.

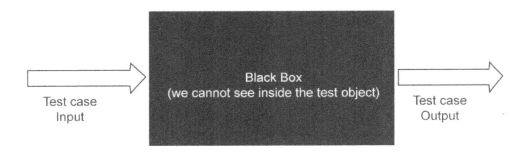

Black-box testing

These techniques concentrate on the inputs and outputs of the test object without reference to its internal structure. They can be used for both functional and non-functional testing.

Test conditions, test cases, and test data are derived from a test basis that may include software requirements, specifications, use cases, etc. This testing is performed by the testers.

White-box test techniques (also called structural or structure-based techniques) are based on an analysis of the architecture, detailed design, internal structure, or the code of the test object.

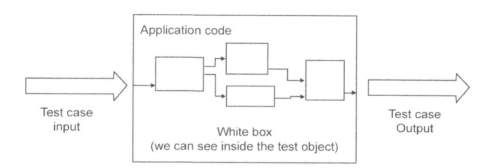

White-box testing

These techniques focus on the structure of the test object. Test conditions, test cases, and test data are derived from a test basis that may include code, software architecture, detailed design, or any other source of information regarding the structure of the software. This testing is performed by the developers.

Experience-based test techniques leverage the experience of developers, testers, and users to design, implement, and execute tests.

Experience-based testing

Black-box and white-box testing may also be combined with experience-based techniques to leverage the experience of developers, testers, and users to determine what should be tested. The knowledge and experience of people (e.g. testers, developers, users, and other stakeholders) are used to derive the test cases. This includes:

- Knowledge of the usage of the software
- Knowledge of the environment of software
- Knowledge about likely defects and their distribution.

Experienced-based techniques would commonly be used to augment more structured test techniques. They are often used when there is no test basis which can be used to create test cases or they are not sufficient. For example, a tester based on his experience might use a surname of 'Roger-water' or 'O'Neal' to test whether these special characters are permitted within the name field in the system.

4   **Defect**

Software systems are increasingly complex, often systems are connected to many other systems. Development of these complex systems requires a great deal of time, skill and effort and during this process, human beings can make **errors or mistakes.**

These **ERRORS** can lead to the introduction of a defect (fault or bug) in the software code or some other related work product. For example, a requirements elicitation error can lead to a requirements defect, which then results in a programming error that leads to a defect in the code.

If a **DEFECT** has been introduced into the code, then after the code is executed it could cause a **FAILURE.** If this happens then the defect has led to a failure. A failure occurs within the system.

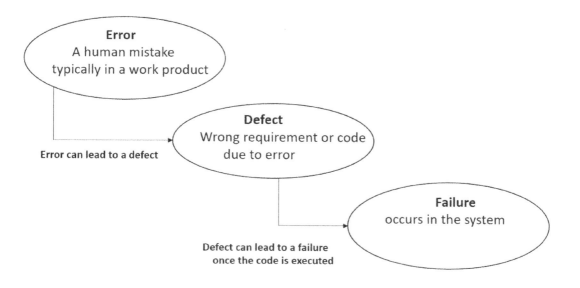

Error, defect and failure

When the tester encounters a bug, they create a defect report, describing what happened and steps to replicate the defect. Later it is decided who is responsible for fixing this failure.

The actual defect correction is a task for the development team. They debug the code to find the root cause and fix the problem. Once it is done the tester will verify it again and then close the defect if it is working properly, otherwise, it will be re-opened again.

Testing cannot directly remove defects, nor can it directly enhance quality. By reporting defects, it makes their removal possible and so contributes to the enhanced quality of the system. In addition, the systematic coverage of a software product in testing allows at least some aspects of the quality of the software to be measured. Testing is one component in the overall quality assurance activity that seeks to ensure that systems go live without defects that can lead to serious failures.

Defect workflow

Defect workflow is the life cycle of a defect. It describes the states of the defect from its creation to the closure.

When a defect is detected as part of testing by a tester, all required data is gathered which can help in a quick resolution of the defect.

Once the defect is raised then it typically progresses through a workflow and sequence of states of defect lifecycle. In most of these states, one of the project team members owns the defect. They are responsible for carrying out a task which when completed, will move the defect to the next state and assigned it to another team member. Most testing organizations use a tool that can manage defects through the defect lifecycle.

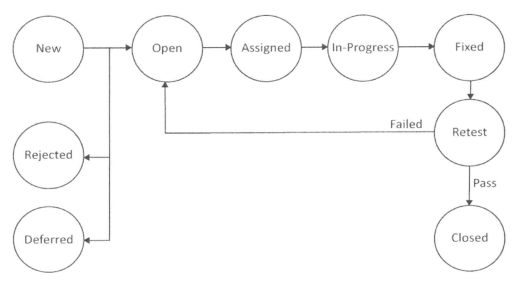

Defect Life Cycle

The following states are there in the defect cycle:

New

When a defect is created, it is assigned a default status of 'New'. While creating the defects test analyst should enter the severity and priority according to their understanding and guess what probably caused the problem based on their experience.

During the defect Triage which is attended by representatives from the Development Team, the Business Analyst Team and the Testing Team, all the defects with 'New' Status are triaged for their validity, severity, and priority. If the defect is considered as a valid one, then the status is changed to 'Open' state and ownership is decided else it is changed to 'Rejected' State. Generally, the Test Lead or Senior Testers represent the testing team in the triage and actively participate in the discussion.

Open

When the defect is accepted as a valid one the status is changed to 'Open'. The development lead will assign the defect to the appropriate developer based on the workload or complexity.

Rejected

When the defect is agreed as an invalid one in the triage meeting the status is changed to 'Rejected' Status.

Assigned

When the defect is assigned to a team member (i.e. the developer) to work on the status is changed to 'Assigned'. The Assigned to field will have details of that team member's name and/or associated userID.

In Progress

When the assignee starts working on the defect, they will change the status from 'Assigned' to 'In Progress' to reflect that.

Fixed

When the code changes required to fix the defect have completed the status of the defect is changed to 'Fixed'. The developer should enter the root cause and the phase when the defect was introduced in the defect details while investigating, debugging, and fixing the defect.

Retest

Testers would change the status to 'Retest' before testing them again. Test lead should monitor if the defects are sitting in retest for a long time and try to find and remove any issues which may be impacting the retesting activity e.g. issues related to test data and environment.

Open/Reopen

If the defect fails the testing, the defect is moved again to 'Open'/Reopen status.

Closed

If the defect passes the testing, the defect is changed to 'Closed' status. When confirming the fix, the tester should verify the root cause setting entered by the developer along with the phase in which the defect was introduced.

Deferred

Defect status can be changed to Deferred to indicate that the defect can be fixed in the future releases.

If the defect tracking tool is used, team members based on their role and access can only change certain defect statuses.

New→ Open/New→Rejected: Test Lead, Development Lead, Business Analyst

Open→Assigned: Development Lead, Business Analyst

Assigned→ In Progress: The team member who is assigned the defect

In progress→Fixed: Developers/ Business Analyst

Fixed→Retest: Testing team members

Retest→Reopen: Testing team members

Retest→Closed: Testing team members

The defects raised during static testing of the requirements are fixed by the business analysts (correcting the documents) and the defects raised during dynamic testing are fixed by the developers (correcting the code).

Defect Triage

Defect Triage is a meeting to discuss the defects raised by testers during scheduled test execution. They are attended by representatives from the Development, Testing and Business Analyst teams. The main focus of this meeting is to verify the validity, severity, and priority of the new defects so the team can work together to fix the most critical defects. By the end of this meeting, effective planning is formulated to deal with the defects discussed during the meeting.

The defect management committee determines whether each defect report represents a valid defect and whether it should be fixed or deferred. This decision requires the defect management committee to consider the benefits, risks, and costs associated with fixing or not fixing the defect. If the defect is to be fixed, the team should establish the priority of fixing the defect relative to other project tasks. The Test Lead and test team are consulted regarding the relative importance of a defect and should provide available objective information. If the defects are not valid then a decision is made to reject those defects.

Defect Severity

Severity is used to determine the impact of a defect on the business function and/or test execution.

Following are the different severity levels used for testing:

Rating	Description	Example
1	Critical	A component of the system is not working or unusable. There is no alternative available. No testing can continue.
2	High	A component of the system is not working or unusable, the impact is critical, but an alternative is available. Limited testing can continue.
3	Medium	The functionality of a component of the system is restricted. There is no critical impact but can have some operational impact. Testing for unrelated areas can continue.
4	Low	There is no operational impact. Testing can continue.

For example, the system under test is an airline website that is used to book online flight tickets. Users can search for the flight by selecting dates and book them based on availability. Tickets can be purchased using Amex, Master, and Visa credit cards via a payment gateway.

Critical defects – Payment gateway not working, search not displaying results, the main website is down.

Major defects – Users can't book the flight using Amex credit cards but booking can be completed using Master and Visa cards.

Medium defects – After the payment on the booking page the option to save ticket as pdf is not displaying.

Minor defects – Spelling mistakes for the static text on the booking main page which don't create any major confusion for the customer.

Defect Priority

The priority of the defects indicates the importance or urgency to fix a defect. The defects which are blocking the execution of other test cases have high priority.

Following are the examples of different priority level used for testing:

Rating	Description	Examples of fix time
1	Urgent	1 business day
2	High	2 business day
3	Medium	3-5 business day
4	Low	Negotiable

The SLA to fix the defects for different priority depends on the project. It should be part of the Test plan document and agreed by all the stakeholders.

Defect Metadata

All the fields which are required to effectively understand, investigate, fix and retest the defects are Defect Metadata. If the defect management tool is used, then to ensure the testers provide this information these fields should be made as mandatory fields. In the absence of a tool, the defect template should be used with the Defect Metadata.

Defect Metadata	Description
Defect ID	An identification number to uniquely identify each defect
Defect Type	Categories defects as static, functional or non-functional
Environment	The environment where the defect is detected
Severity	Impact of defect on test execution and/or business function
Priority	Defect classification which indicates the urgency or importance to fix the defect
Data Raised	The date when the defect was found
Summary	The high-level description of the defect
Steps to Reproduce	Detailed steps to replicate the defects (e.g. Step 1: Log in to the system using customer id: xx123, Step2: Click on Transfer button)
Expected Result	The expected results of the test (e.g. Transfer page is displayed)
Actual results	The actual results of the test (e.g. Error page is displayed)
Reference	Reference to Test case or Requirement
Evidence	Evidence of defect (e.g. screenshots, attachments, SQL query results)

5 Fundamental Test Process

Testing is not an ad hoc activity in the project lifecycle but a process which runs in parallel to other project activities. A common perception of software testing is that it only consists of running tests, i.e. executing the software under given test conditions. This is a misconception because while running tests is part of testing but that doesn't constitute all of the testing activities. Test activities exist before and after test execution – activities such as planning and control, choosing test conditions, designing test cases and checking results, evaluating completion criteria, reporting on the testing process and the system under test, and closure activities.

This chapter will cover the activities which are followed as part of the test process, based on the software development model used in the project these testing activities are planned and executed.

The test process consists of the following main groups of activities:

- Test planning
- Test monitoring and control
- Test analysis
- Test design
- Test implementation
- Test execution
- Test completion

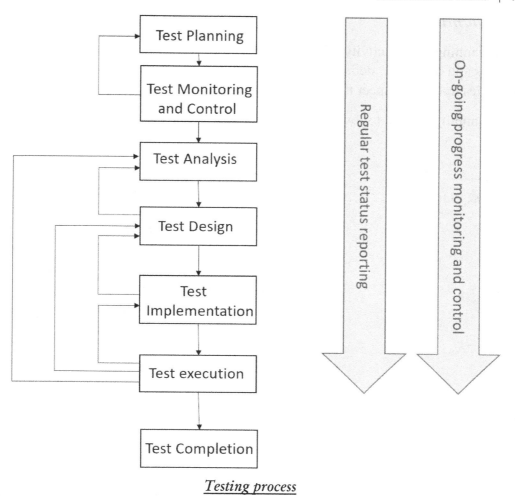

Testing process

Each group of main activities is composed of constituent activities which may consist of multiple individual tasks. These tasks would vary from one project or release to another.

Further, some of these main activity groups may appear logically sequential but they are often implemented iteratively or tailored based on the context of the system and project.

Test planning

Test planning is the activity of planning about the testing activities, coming up with the mission of testing, defining the objectives of testing and the specification of test activities in order to meet the objectives and mission.

Test planning has the following major tasks:

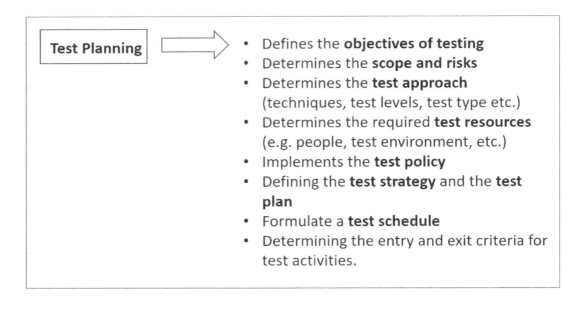

Test Planning ⟹
- Defines the **objectives of testing**
- Determines the **scope and risks**
- Determines the **test approach** (techniques, test levels, test type etc.)
- Determines the required **test resources** (e.g. people, test environment, etc.)
- Implements the **test policy**
- Defining the **test strategy** and the **test plan**
- Formulate a **test schedule**
- Determining the entry and exit criteria for test activities.

Note
The majority of Test planning tasks are done by Test lead or Test Manager based on the inputs from testers.

Test monitoring and control

Test monitoring and control include the **on-going activities** of **comparing actual progress against the planned progress** and reporting the status, including deviations from the plan. They involve taking actions necessary to meet the mission and objectives of the project. In order to control testing, progress should be monitored throughout the project.

Test monitoring and control have the following major tasks:

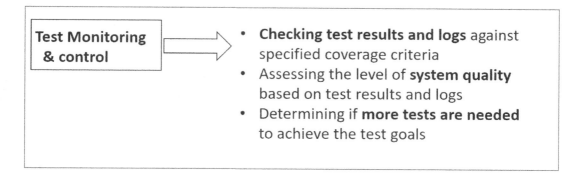

```
┌─────────────────┐
│ Test Monitoring │ ──────▷   • Checking test results and logs against
│ & control       │             specified coverage criteria
└─────────────────┘           • Assessing the level of system quality
                                based on test results and logs
                              • Determining if more tests are needed
                                to achieve the test goals
```

Note
The majority of Test Monitoring and control tasks are done by Test lead or Test Manager based on the inputs from testers.

Test analysis

Test analysis is the activity where requirements are reviewed and high-level test cases (test conditions) are created based on that.

It has the following major tasks:

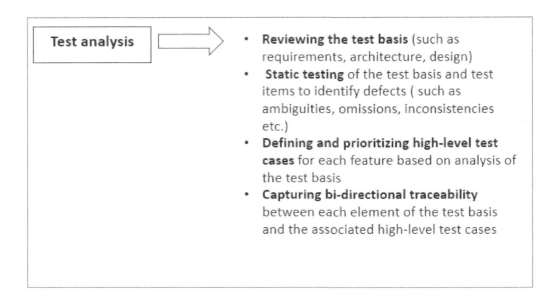

Test analysis	

- **Reviewing the test basis** (such as requirements, architecture, design)
- **Static testing** of the test basis and test items to identify defects (such as ambiguities, omissions, inconsistencies etc.)
- **Defining and prioritizing high-level test cases** for each feature based on analysis of the test basis
- **Capturing bi-directional traceability** between each element of the test basis and the associated high-level test cases

Note
The majority of the Test analysis tasks are done by testers.

Test design

Test design is the activity where high-level test cases are transformed into low-level test cases.

It has the following major tasks:

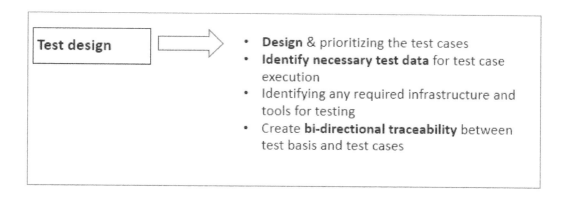

As with test analysis, test design can also have a potential benefit of the identification of similar types of defects in the test basis.

Note
The majority of the Test design tasks are done by testers.

Test implementation

Test implementation is the activity where test suites are created from the test cases.

It has the following major tasks:

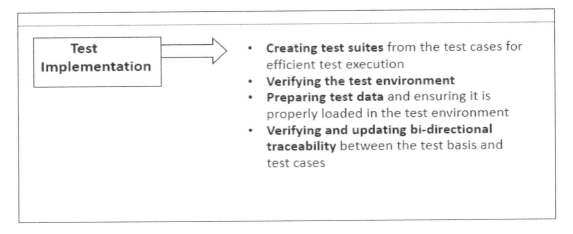

Test execution

Test execution is the activity where test cases are run. It has the following major tasks:

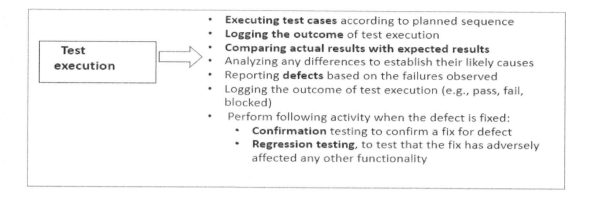

Test completion

Test completion activities occur at project milestones such as when a software system is released, a test project is completed (or cancelled) or a test level is completed.

Test completion has the following major tasks:

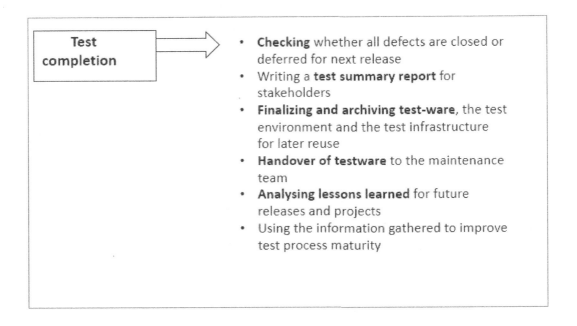

Note
The majority of test completion tasks are done together by Test Lead/Test Manager and testers.

6 | Test Case Preparation

As we discussed in the previous chapter test case preparation and test execution are the major tasks for testers. In this chapter, we will check in detail how the test cases are prepared. This is part of the test analysis and test design of the testing process discussed earlier. Before the testers start formal testing, they create test cases based on the specifications (requirements docs, functional specs, design documents, etc.). The work-products that are used to create the test cases are called **test basis**.

A test case is a sequence of steps, to test the behavior of functionality or feature of a system. An expected result is usually given with the set of variables (test data) to use for testing. Based on this test case execution tester will determine whether the system is working according to the specifications or requirements.

How to design test cases

Let's take an example of a web-based project which has the following specification for a customer input screen:

The input screen shall have three fields:

- A title field with a drop-down selector.
- The last name field that can accept up to 25 alphabetic characters and the apostrophe (') character.
- A first name field which can accept up to 25 alphabetic characters.

The rules for these fields are:

- All fields are mandatory, which means they should be completed.
- All alphabetic characters entered are case insensitive.
- The data is validated when the user leaves a particular field or tab out
- If the data for all the field are valid, the next page (financial input screen) is displayed .
- If the data for any of these fields are invalid, an error message is displayed, and the user stays on the same page.

These specifications enables us to define test conditions or high-level test scenario; for example, we could define a test condition for the last name field (i.e. it can accept up to 25 alphabetic characters including the apostrophe (') character) and define a set of test cases to test that field.

To test the **last name** field, first, we need to be on the appropriate input screen, select a title and then navigate to the last name field (all these are pre-condition for the test). Now, we enter a value in the last name field (the first set of input values), then, navigate to the first name field and enter a value (the second set of input values that we need because all fields must be completed) and then press the Enter key. If the input data is valid the financial input screen will be displayed otherwise, there will be an error message for invalid data. So, we would need to test both of these scenarios.

The preceding paragraph is effectively the test case, just we will put them in a step by step procedure, so it is easy for the tester to follow the steps for real testing.

A good test case needs some extra information. First, it should be traceable back to the test condition and the element of the specification that it is testing; Secondly, we need to add test data used for testing e.g. Mr. Roger Roll, Finally, we would specify that the system should move to the financial input screen when the user press 'Enter' button.

TEST CASE DESIGN EXAMPLE

As an example, we can use the following test data for our test cases:

Mr Roger	Roll
Ms Hari	Xyzffyuuuuqwertyuik
Ms ABCDEdfafklkoermnoert	samar
Mr James	O'Hare

All these are positive test cases; even though the name ABCDEdfafklkoermnoert and last name Xyzffyuuuuqwertyuik don't look like a real first name and last name but the input is correct according to the specification.

Testing should also cover negative scenarios with invalid inputs, such as:

Mr Thomas77	$ummer
Mr "Morgan"	Peter-ras
Ms Ruma$	'Niel&

There are many more scenarios we can create that could generate a very large number of test cases. One of the aims of testing is to achieve the desired coverage and level of confidence by just the minimum number of test cases.

The low-level test case would look like the following:

TC ID	TC Name	Step No.	Test Step Description	Expected Results
TC_01	Validate last name field	Step1	Launch the system	System is launched
		Step2	Select the "Personal Details" option from the main menu	"Personal Details" screen is displayed
		Step3	Select 'Mr.' from the 'Title' drop-down menu	The title is selected and the cursor moves to the 'last name' field
		Step4	Type in 'Roshan' and press the tab key once	The cursor moves to the 'first name' field.
		Step5	Type in 'Raj' and press the Enter key.	The financial input screen is displayed.

This is just one of the positive test scenarios, similarly, we need to create the negative test scenarios.

A typical test case has the following fields (but not limited to):

- **Test case ID** – To uniquely identify the test case
- **Test priority**– This will help to decide on the sequence of the run, high priority test cases are related to the high-risk areas or critical business functions which should be executed first.
- **Pre-condition**– Any preconditions before running the test. E.g. Account page can be tested after the user has successfully logged in to the system.
- **Requirement Id-** Link to the requirement which the test covers.
- **Dependencies**- If this test case is dependent on other test cases. E.g. The Interest statement can be tested after the End Of Month batch run is successfully completed.
- **Test Steps**– Detailed step by step information to help in executing the test case.

  E.g. step 1: open webpage www.banktest.com,
  step 2: Enter user id and password and click on the Login button

- **Test Data** – Test variable to be used for testing. E.g. **user id**: AD345 **password**: abcd#1234
- **Expected Result-** Final result the tester can verify after going through the test steps e.g. confirmation page displayed with current date and time.

Following fields are added before the test case execution

- **Actual result**– The actual behavior of the application/system under test with test data
- **Status (Pass/Fail)**– If the actual result is the same as expected result, then the status will be **Pass** otherwise it will be **Fail**. The status can also be **blocked** (due to defect) or **not executed** (waiting execution).
- **Defect #-** If the status is Fail, there will be corresponding defect # in the field to link the test case to the defect. Once the defect is fixed the test case needs to be executed again.

There are other fields to record the name of the tester who has created the test cases and the name of the tester who has executed the test case with execution date/time. If a test management tool is used it will automatically populate these details based on the login details of the tester.

Black box Test techniques

In **black-box testing**, the system is viewed as a **'black box'**, in the sense that the box is opaque, and its internal activity is therefore not visible to the tester. The tester concentrates on the inputs and outputs of the system without reference to its internal structure.

In **Black-box test techniques** (also called behavioral or behavior-based techniques) test cases are designed based on the analysis of the test basis documentation and reflect the specified behavior of the system under test.

Following two techniques are quite popular for selecting the appropriate number of test cases for black-box testing especially for ST/SIT testing.

- Equivalence Partitioning
- Boundary Value Analysis

Equivalence Partitioning is a test design technique that divides the inputs and outputs of a system into **different classes or partitions**. Selecting **one value** from each partition will ensure the coverage for all the values from that partition.

Most of the systems contain a large number of possible inputs and outputs. Testing the system considering all of them is nearly impossible. In such cases, the technique of equivalence partitioning may be helpful as it assists the tester in defining the reduced number of test cases that can effectively test the system.

Partitioning is used to create equivalence classes (often called equivalence partitions) which are sets of values that are processed in the same manner. By selecting one representative value from a partition, coverage for all the items in the same partition is assumed.

Example:

A bank allows the customers to apply for an online bank account. The customer age is taken as input and if the customer age is between 18 to 60 years they can proceed with the online application. The customer age field only accepts integer values greater than zero.

If we use the equivalence partitioning technique to test this system, we can divide the input (customer age) into three equivalence classes or partitions as shown below.

We can take any one of the values from each equivalence class. E.g. 15, 20, 65. Thus, three test cases will be sufficient.

In this case, the values from the first and third partitions are invalid values and values from the second partitions are valid values.

If there is a slight variation in the requirement and the system accepts any integers, then the partitions will increase. There will be one partition to test negative values (age entered with '-' sign) and one partition to test age entered as zero.

So, to verify all the equivalence classes we will need five test cases. They will check the system with (-15), (0), (15), (20), (65) (one value from each partition)

Boundary Value Analysis (BVA) is an extension of equivalence partitioning but can only be used when the partition is ordered, consisting of numeric or sequential data. **The first and last value of a partition is its boundary values**.

Behavior at the boundaries of equivalence partitions is more likely to be incorrect than behavior within the partitions. In most of the cases, both specified and implemented boundaries may be displaced to positions above or below their intended positions, may be omitted altogether, or maybe supplemented with unwanted additional boundaries. Boundary value analysis and testing will reveal almost all such defects by forcing the software to show behaviors from a partition other than the one to which the boundary value should belong.

There are two ways to approach BVA: **two value** or **three value** testing. With **two value testing**, the **boundary value** (on the boundary) and the value that is just **over the boundary** (by the smallest possible increment) are used. For **three value** boundary testing, the values **before**, **on** and **over the boundary** are used. The values are based on the risk associated with the item being tested, with the **three-boundary approach being used for the higher risk items.**

For both Equivalence Partitioning and Boundary Value Analysis, the output values of the set classes also need an examination to ensure that they are valid.

If we use the online bank account example discussed earlier and use the boundary value analysis to test this system, we need to first divide the input (customer age) into three equivalence classes or partitions as shown below.

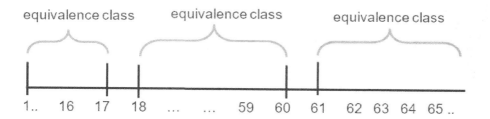

For the second equivalence class, the first and last value of the partitions are the boundary values

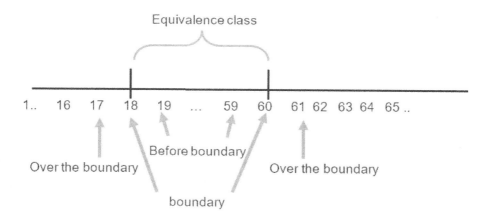

The two-point boundary value requires that 2 values are tested at each boundary; **one on the boundary** and **one 'just' over the boundary**. (i.e. 17, 18 and 60, 61)

The three-point boundary value requires that 3 values are tested at each boundary; **one 'just' before the boundary, one on the boundary** and **one 'just' over the boundary**. (i.e. 19, 18, 17 and 59, 60, 61)

Boundary value analysis can be applied at all test levels. The values are based on the risk associated with the item being tested, with the three-boundary approach being used for the higher risk items. It is relatively easy to apply and its defect finding capability is high. Boundary value and equivalence partitioning are usually used together to design test cases.

7   **Environments**

As discussed earlier different test phases are carried out in different environments. A typical project will use the following environment for software development activities:

- **Development (DEV)**

  This environment is used for all development activities for projects which includes the component and component integration testing.

- **TEST**

  This environment is used by the testing team for System Testing (ST), System Integration Testing (SIT) and regression testing. This environment should be connected to the external systems so the End to End testing can be performed.

- **UAT**

  This environment is used by business users or customer representative for the Business Verification testing (BV) or User Acceptance Testing (UAT) after the other testing phases are complete. This environment should be similar to the production environment with similar data so the defects which are related to data and environment can be found here.

- **Production (PROD)**

  This environment is used for the final release of the project and the PIV/PVT testing.

In some organization, there is a separate environment (**PRE-PROD**) which can be used for carrying out any non-functional testing i.e. performance testing and to fix and test any production-related issues. In the absence of this environment, the UAT environment can also be used to test any production-related issues or for any non-functional testing.

8 Tools used by Testing Team

To support the testing activities testing team can use tools. These can be used to support one or more testing activities. Such tools include:

- Tools that are directly used in testing, such as test execution tools and test data preparation tools.
- Tools that are used for reporting and monitoring test execution, and managing requirements, manual and automated test cases, test results, test data, and defects.
- Tools that are used for investigation and evaluation.
- Tools that assist in testing e.g. a spreadsheet is also a test tool if it used to support any of the tests activity.

Following is the list of the most common tools used by the testing team.

Test Management tool (e.g. ALM (Application Life Cycle Management), QC (Quality Center))

- These tools support for the overall test management activities of the project
- Have capability for in-build test execution, defect tracking and requirement management tools or interfaces to other tools which can provide this capability
- Independent version control or interface with an external configuration management tool
- Support for traceability of tests, test results and defects to source documents, such as requirement specifications
- Logging of test results and generation of progress reports
- Quantitative analysis (metrics) related to the tests (e.g., tests run, tests passed) and the test object (e.g., defects raised)

Defect management tool/Defect tracking tool (e.g. JIRA, Bugzilla)

- Store and manage defects.
- Facilitate the prioritization of defects.
- Allow defect assignment to different team members for actions required (e.g., developer to fix or to the tester for confirmation test).
- Attribution of status (e.g. rejected, ready to be tested, or deferred to next release).
- Provide support for statistical analysis and the creation of defect reports.

Test data preparation tools (e.g. AdvancedMiner)

- These tools analyze the requirements document or source code to determine the data required during testing to achieve a level of coverage.
- Some of the advanced tools take a data set from a production system and "scrub" or "anonymize" it to remove any personal information while still maintaining the internal integrity of that data. The scrubbed data can then be used for testing without the risk of a security leak or misuse of personal information. This is particularly important where large volumes of realistic data are required.
- Some of these tools can generate test data from given sets of input parameters (i.e., for use in random testing) or analyze the database structure to determine what inputs will be required from the testers.

Performance testing tools (e.g. Performance Center, LoadRunner, Jmeter)

- These tools are used to assess system performance.
- They can be used to simulate a load on an application, or a database, or a network or server.
- Monitor and report on how a system behaves under a variety of simulated usage conditions.

Test comparators (e.g. Beyond Compare)

- These tools are used to compare large data files or raw data.
- These tools can identify differences between the actual results produced by the system and the expected results of a test.
- These tools are used mostly during the testing of the large database migration projects where testers have to compare the data stored in different tables between the old and the new databases.

Test Automation Tool (e.g. QTP (Quick Test Professional), UFT (Unified Functional Tester), Selenium)

- These tools allow the automation of user actions on a web or client-based system.
- These tools use some scripting language to record objects, control, and user actions. In most cases, technical expertise in the scripting language is necessary for the tester.
- Later these tests can be executed automatically using a different range of stored inputs. For example, running the test with different customer data stored in the files.
- There is an ability to manipulate the tests with limited effort. For example, to repeat the test with different data or to test a different part of the system with similar steps.
- They can record the screenshots during the execution as part of the test log which can be used later in case there are any failures and for auditing purposes.

Note
Selenium is an **open-source tool** for automation and is quite popular for testing web applications nowadays. It is a suite of tools that can be used for automating any browser-based application. It supports automation testing of functional aspects as well as UI testing of a web application across a variety of platforms.   Selenium runs on many browsers and operating systems, and Selenium test scripts can be written in a variety of programming languages. Due to its cross-browser and cross-platform testing capability, it is used widely in the industry for regression testing.

9 | **Skills for Software Tester**

To successfully perform the job of software testers, the following skills are required:

- Skills to perform basic testing duties (Technical skills)
- Skills required to work in a team environment (Soft skills)

Technical skills

It's nearly impossible for a tester to survive in the profession without sound technical skills. Some of the attributes which contribute to the tester's technical knowledge base are:

Knowledge of testing activities

This helps the testers in analyzing the requirements and design test cases, and the diligence for running tests and recording the results. This will also help in understanding the existing testing process and the defect tracking process.

Testing of similar application/systems

Testers who have testing experience of similar software applications/systems have a better understanding of how the system works, where failures would have the greatest impact, and how the system should react in various situations. All this knowledge helps in the planning and execution of the testing activities.

Participation in various phases of software development

Knowledge of the software development lifecycle/process (requirements analysis, architecture, design, and coding) gives insight into which testing activities can be started during each phase and how errors lead to the introduction of defects, where defects can be detected and how to prevent the introduction of defects in the first place.

Business domain Knowledge

Testers with domain expertise know which areas are of most importance to the business and how those areas affect the ability of the business to meet its requirements. This knowledge can be used to verify and understand the requirements, create realistic test cases and test data and prioritize the test cases for execution.

Note
After going through the book, you will get a good understanding of testing activities that can be applied for testing real systems. You will also understand how testing activities are performed for a system in the banking domain.

Soft skills

Testers can't succeed in their career with just strong technical skills, they should also possess and employ the necessary soft skills. Soft skills help the testers to work more effectively both in the workplace and with others. Testers who possess these traits not only become the best testers, but they also grow quickly in their careers.

Following are the various soft skills that a tester should possess to be successful:

Communication

It is required to carry on the daily testing tasks in a team environment. The communication can be within the testing team or with other stakeholders. For a tester, both verbal and written communication is crucial. Testers must be attentive to detail and possess strong written and verbal communication skills. Testers should have the ability to describe a scenario or situations to other stakeholders. For example, how to recreate a complicated defect.

Interpersonal skills

Interpersonal skills, such as giving and receiving constructive criticism, influencing, and negotiating are all important skills to play the role of a tester and work effectively with other members of the project team.

Time management and prioritization of work

Testers should be able to define the importance given to each task and the sequence in which they should be performed. These skills help the tester to manage their work better.

Listening

During the discussions/meetings, testers should be able to interpret what the stakeholders are talking about and turn those into actions.

Right attitude

It enhances tester's ability to quickly learn new things and develop other effective soft skills.

Note
To be a successful tester you need to work on your soft skills, these skills are required not only for software testing but for any job which involves a team environment.

10 Applying Testing in the Context of Project

To apply testing in the context of a project let's consider the testing for a fictitious bank named "Global Sun" which in no way related to any real entity with the same or similar name.

The Global Sun bank is one of the growing consumer bank (retail bank) responsible for sales and service of around 1.2 million customers in Australia. To assist the customers for their everyday banking needs activities are conducted through the Global Sun bank's nationwide network of branches, call centers, ATM terminals, and internet banking services.

Typical products offered by a Global Sun bank include **savings and transactional accounts**, **mortgages** and **credit cards**. Following are the details for the products:

Transactional accounts-Checking accounts or Current accounts

It is a deposit account held at a bank. It is available to the account owner "on-demand" and is available for frequent and immediate access by the account owner. Access may be in a variety of ways, such as cash withdrawals using branches or ATMs, use of cheques (checks) and debit by electronic transfer.

Savings accounts

A savings account is a deposit account held at a retail bank that pays interest but cannot be used directly as transactional accounts. These accounts let customers set aside a portion of their liquid assets while earning a monetary return.

Credit card

A credit card is a payment card issued to cardholders which allows them to borrow money from a bank under the agreement that you'll repay it by the bill's due date or incur interest charges. Credit cards allow customers to make purchases without using your own money.

Mortgage Account

A mortgage Account is used by purchasers to buy real estate. The loan is "secured" on the borrower's property which means that a legal mechanism is put in place which allows the lender to take possession and sell the secured property to pay off the loan if the borrower defaults on the loan.

Note
A typical bank will have many more products for customers but for ease of understanding, we are only considering these four products for our project.

11 Problem Statement and Solution for Global Sun Bank

Before the project is kickstarted the project manager and higher management will analyze the problem statement and present the IT solution to the sponsors of the project and stakeholders. These tasks are part of project initiation and mostly involve business teams and managers. Once the solution is approved by sponsors of the project a budget is allocated and the project starts. Testers and other project team members are not involved in most of these activities, but knowledge of this will give you a good perspective on the drivers for IT projects.

The proposal will look something like this…

Currently, the Global Sun customers must visit bank branches to do International money transfer which is a tedious and time-consuming activity. Most of the Global Sun competitors are having online banking solutions. Global Sun should develop a new solution, so the customers can perform International Money Transfer (IMT) via Global Sun Online banking site. The money will be transferred electronically from the customer Global Sun account to the overseas account within 2-3 business days. The customer should be able to send money to over 99 countries without visiting the branch by directly using this online IMT system.

According to the IMT proposal, the IMT Program will provide the following benefits:

- **Fast Electronic Transfer**– The money is transferred electronically from the Global Sun account to the overseas account within 2-3 business days.

- **Real-time market rates**- While transferring via Global Sun Internet Banking customers can see the real-time market rates for forex and they can take advantage of exchange rate movements during the day and lock in the rate that suits them.

- **Staff independent service** – Customers can perform this entire transfer from their online banking site without any interaction with bank staff.

This system will reduce customer dependency on bank staff. This will result in saving for the bank in the long run. Return on Investment (ROI) is displayed below for the Global Sun IMT project which shows that after year three, Global Sun will get back the payout for the investment in the IMT project.

ROI Calculator - for IT system projects
Project name: SunBank IMT project

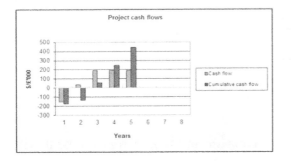

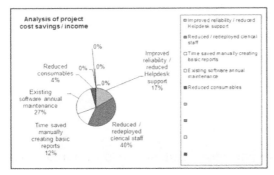

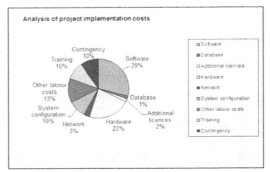

Results Summary		
Total project cost savings/income $'000		845
Total project expenditures	$'000	-403
Net project savings / income	$'000	442
ROI (return on investment - after 5 years)		109.7%
NPV (net present value)	$' 000	241
at a discount rate of		12.0%
IRR (internal rate of return)		56.3%
Payback year		Year 3

Note

For a typical IT project, **ROI** is calculated to justify the cost of investment. In most cases, upper management approves the investment in the IT solution based on the cost-saving to the business in the long run or to be competitive in the market. The same factors are applicable to the IMT project.

12 Current and Future State Architecture

The architecture diagram is the pictorial representation of the system with details of the internal component and their interactions and dataflow. These diagrams are prepared by architects or designers and are part of the design document. These design documents are used by the developers to understand the overall architecture and for creating component and technical specifications documents. These are also useful for the testers to get a clear picture of the overall system and use that information for planning for their testing. These diagrams help to find out how the different components within the overall system are connected and the connectivity with any external systems. Based on this information the testers can plan for the System Integration Testing (SIT). These diagrams can help to understand the downstream system risks. (how the data flow of the system can affect the systems which are using it as an input)

The following diagram show the current state for the Global Sun online banking system.

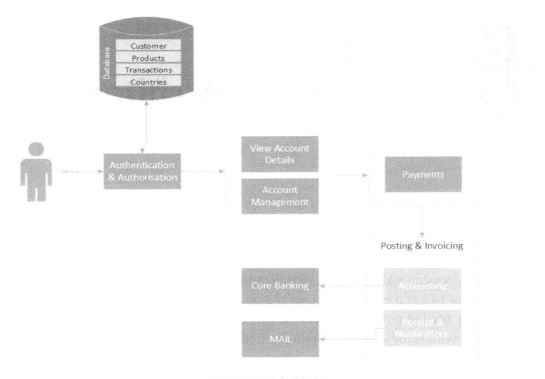

CURRENT STATE

The following diagram shows the future state for the Global Sun online banking system with IMT changes:

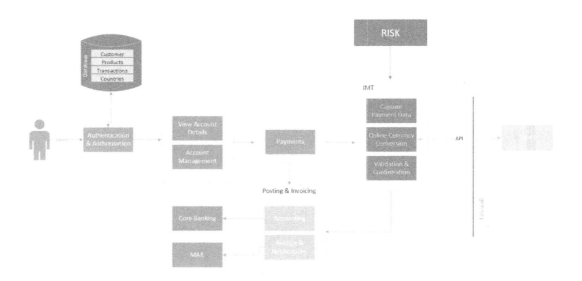

FUTURE STATE AFTER IMT CHANGES

Note

The new IMT system will get data-feed from an internal Global Sun system called RISK which will send the data for the list of countries on the sanctions list (not eligible for international transfers), the minimum and maximum limit for transfers and UpToDate terms and conditions, etc. This information will come to the RISK system from other systems or entered manually by the RISK system team.

The New IMT system is also connected to the SWIFT system. The current currency exchange rates are received in real-time from SWIFT and once the customer confirms the international payment it is converted to a SWIFT message and sent to the SWIFT system which acts as a network for the financial institutions.

13 Project Stakeholders

Once the proposed solution is approved by Global Sun management, the project can be started. Now different project stakeholders start working on their respective project activities.

The testing team interact with the following stakeholders for various test activities during the project lifecycle. These stakeholders may vary depending on the project and the organization.

- **Business Analyst (BA)** works with the end-users or business users to determine the user requirement for the software. They are responsible for creating a business requirement document (BRD) based on the user requirement. The testing team interacts with them to get the understanding of requirements which enable them to create high-level test cases (test conditions) and low-level test cases (detailed test cases). The test cases created by the testing team are also reviewed by the Business Analyst for completeness. They provide inputs to the testing team on all the testing artifacts i.e. test strategy, test plan, test results, reports.

- **Development Lead/Development Manager** manages the developers in the project and is responsible for the delivery of the software. During testing the team interacts with them regarding the build status and deployment schedules. They represent the development team in different meetings especially during defect triage discussions and provide inputs to the testing team on all the testing artifacts i.e. test strategy, test plan, test results, reports.

- **Developers/Programmer** writes the software code and performs unit and unit integration testing. During the test execution, they work closely with testers to fix the defects.

- **Database Architects, System architects, and solution designers** are responsible for creating the Solution Design Document (SDD) or Technical Design Document (TDD). These documents describe the design of the system and integration between different components and interfaces which can help in understanding the overall solution and plan for integration testing. The testing team interacts with them to get an understanding of the overall solution which can help them design their tests for System Integration Testing (SIT).

- **End users/ business users** use the software directly or indirectly. They provide the requirements to the BA. They perform UAT/BV testing phase to make sure that software is fit for the purpose. The testing team may provide support or assist them during the UAT testing phase.

- **Operations/Technical support team** they are responsible for building and maintaining the test and the production environment. They facilitate final code deployment to the production environment on the project release date.

- **Project Manager (PM)** manages the overall project and resourcing. They include the efforts of testing activities and the testing milestones in the project plan. They keep a close eye on the testing report and results to make sure the project meet the milestone dates.

14 Testing Team Structure

A typical testing team has the following team members who perform different activities based on their skills and experience. These roles and responsibilities may vary based on the organization and also on the size and complexity of the project.

- Test Manager
- Test Lead
- Senior Test Analyst/ Senior Tester
- Functional Test Analyst/ Tester
- Automation Test Analyst/ Tester
- Performance Test Analyst/ Tester

Test Manager (TM) takes the overall responsibility for the test process and leadership of the test activities. Typical tasks include:

- Managing the entire testing team for a project or program.
- Close coordination with project stakeholders from the project initiation phase to understand test objectives.
- Participate in the risk analysis sessions with stakeholders and suggesting how testing will mitigate product risks.
- Develop the test strategy for the project or program.
- Plan the testing activities and validate the test estimates and testing plan.
- Decide on the metrics used for measuring test progress and scheduling different testing activities.

Test Lead (TL) manages the testing for the project or a testing phase. Typical tasks include:

- Create test estimates and develop the Test Plan for the project.
- Allocate tasks to the testing team and manage their daily activities.
- Prepare the Test Status Report and Test Summary Report for the stakeholders.

The tasks for Test Manager and Test Lead may vary and overlap based on the project and organization; for small projects, Test Lead may handle all the test management tasks and in a large project, it will be shared between Test Manager and Test Lead.

Senior Test Analyst (STA) is an experienced/senior tester in the project who is having good experience of testing the current system or similar systems. STA is well experienced in testing and has good knowledge of testing processes. Typical tasks include:

- Helping the team in the analyses of requirements and preparation of high-level test cases.
- Review the test cases prepared by other testers
- Training the new testers in the team.
- Taking care of some of the test management activities in the absence of the Test Lead.

Functional Testers/Test Analysts (TA) are responsible for the functional testing of the system. Typical tasks include:

- Analyze the requirements to create high-level test cases (test conditions or test scenarios) and low-level test cases (detailed test cases).
- Identify and find/prepare test data for the testing.
- Execute the test cases and record the test results during test execution.
- Reporting the defects when failures are found during testing, and retesting them once they are fixed by the developers.

Automation Test Analyst/Test Engineer is responsible for automating the manual test cases. They have a good knowledge of the automation tool and the scripting language which is used for automation. Typical tasks include:

- Understanding the manual test cases and automating them using the test automation tool.
- Helping the testing team in choosing the right test cases for automation
- Analysis of the test case to see if it is feasible to automate them
- Maintenance of the automation scripts when there are changes to the system.

Non-Functional Test Analyst is responsible for the performance testing of the system. Typical tasks include:

- Analyze the **non-functional requirements** to create test scenarios/scripts for performance or load tests.
- Run the scripts and monitor the performance of the system, For example checking the performance of the system when 100 users have simultaneously logged into the system.

Non-Functional Test Analyst use system design documents or consult developers/ DBA's/ Architects before creating and running the test scripts for performance testing. Tools are mostly used to perform such testing therefore a good knowledge of these tools is essential for this role.

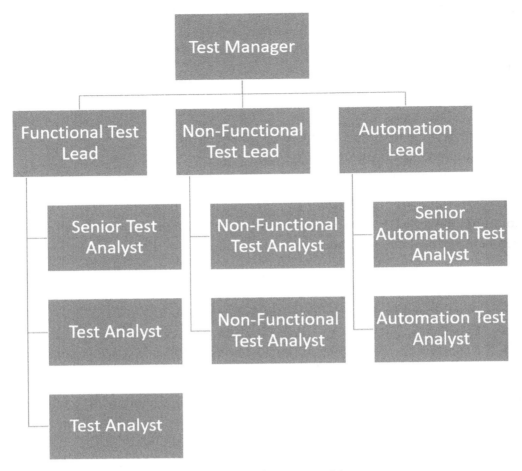

The hierarchy for Testing Team

15 Test Strategy

Some of the common test management documents which are used to manage and plan the testing activities are:

- **Test policy**–Which describes the organization's objectives and goals for testing.
- **Test strategy**–Which describes the overall testing approach for the project or program.
- **Test plan (or project test plan)**–which describes the implementation of the test strategy for a particular project and defines the high level of the test activities being planned. For large projects there can be a master test plan for the whole project and multiple level-specific test plans for each test level.

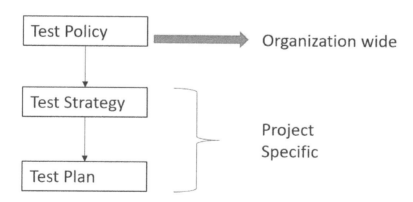

Test Management and Planning Documents

The test strategy outlines the **testing** approach of the project. The test strategy document describes the overall testing approach in detail and provides direction for the testing. This document describes the identified product risk and how these risks will be mitigated by testing, the division of testing into levels, and the high-level activities associated with testing. The test strategy, and the processes and activities described in it, should be consistent with the test policy. It should provide the generic test entry and exit criteria for the organization or for one or more projects or programs.

It is created to inform project stakeholders about testing objectives, key issues of the testing process, methods of testing and test data and environment requirement.

The following should be addressed in the test strategy document in detail.

- Standards to be followed in the project (dependent on the domain of the system under test)
- Test levels to be used (e.g. System test, System integration test, UAT test)
- Test types to be used (such as functional, non-functional testing and experience-based).
- Test design techniques to be used (such as equivalence partitioning, boundary value analysis, etc.).
- Approach to retesting and regression testing
- Entry and exit criteria to be used for each level of testing (such as no outstanding critical defects can be exit criteria for System testing test levels).
- Defect management (including SLA's or timeframe to fix defects).
- Details of test environments to be used for testing
- Tools used to support testing activities

The test strategy also describes the test levels to be carried out including entry and exit criteria for each level and how each level is related. For example, how the test coverage objectives are shared by different levels.

Test strategy also differs based on the development models followed in the project and different test strategies are suitable for different organizations and projects. For example, for a safety-critical system a more intensive strategy may be appropriate.

Following are some of the common test strategies:

Analytical strategies, such as risk-based testing, where tests are designed and prioritized based on the level of risk. This type of test strategy is based on the analysis of some factors (e.g., requirement or risk).

For example, in requirements-based testing the high-level tests are derived from the requirements, low-level tests are then designed and implemented to cover those requirements. The tests are subsequently executed, often using the priority of the requirement covered by each test to determine the order in which the tests will be run. Test results are also reported in terms of requirements status, e.g., requirement tested and passed, requirement tested and failed, etc.

Model-based strategies, such as operational profiling, where the tests are designed on the basis of some model. This model may be built based on the certain required aspect of the product, such as a function, a business process, an internal structure, or a non-functional characteristic (e.g., reliability) or on actual or anticipated situations of the environment in which the product exists.

For example, in model-based performance testing of a growing social media site, testers might develop models to show active and inactive users, and resulting processing load, based on current usage and project growth over time. In addition, models might be developed considering the current production environment's hardware, software, data capacity, network, and infrastructure. Models may also be developed for ideal, expected, and minimum throughput rates, response times, and resource allocation.

Methodical strategies, such as quality characteristic-based, where the test team uses a predetermined set of test conditions, such as based on a quality standard (e.g., ISO 25000), a checklist or a collection of generalized, logical test conditions which may relate to a particular domain, application or type of testing (e.g., security testing), or taxonomy of common or likely types of failures, a list of important quality characteristics, or company-wide look-and-feel standards for mobile apps or web pages.

For example, during maintenance testing of a simple online shopping website, testers might use a checklist that identifies the key functions (new order, modify order, delete orders), attributes, and links for each page. The testers would cover the relevant elements of this checklist each time a modification is made to the site.

Reactive strategies, such as defect-based attacks, where testing is not pre-planned but is reactive to the component or system being tested, and the events occurring during test execution. Tests are designed and implemented, and may immediately be executed in response to knowledge gained from prior test results.

For example, when using exploratory testing on a menu-based application, a set of test charters corresponding to the features, menu selections, and screens might be developed. Each tester is assigned a set of test charters, which they then use to structure their exploratory testing sessions. Testers periodically report the results of the testing sessions to the Test Manager, who may revise the charters based on the findings.

Consultative strategies, such as user-directed testing, where the test team relies on the advice, guidance, or instructions of stakeholders, business domain experts, or technology experts, who may be outside the test team or outside the organization itself.

For example, in outsourced compatibility testing for a web-based application, a company may give the outsourced testing service provider a prioritized list of different browsers and their versions against which they want to evaluate their application.

Regression-averse testing strategy, in which the test strategy is motivated by a desire to avoid regression of existing capabilities. This test strategy includes the reuse of existing testware (especially test cases and test data), extensive automation of regression tests, and standard test suites.

For example, when regression testing, a web-based application, testers can use a GUI-based test automation tool to automate the application. Those tests are then executed at any time the application is modified.

Different strategies may be combined to come up with an appropriate test strategy. For example, risk-based testing (an analytical strategy) can be combined with exploratory testing (a reactive strategy); they complement each other and may achieve more effective testing when used together.

The specific strategies selected should be appropriate to the organization's needs and means, and organizations may tailor strategies to fit operations and projects.

For **IMT** project **Risk-based testing and Regression-averse testing strategy** is selected as it is a banking application where the risk of failure can have a high impact on the bank and customer. Also, it is built on an existing online banking application therefore, regression risk needs to be also reduced to an appropriate level.

For **Risk-based testing**, the test team will design the tests based on the analysis of the identified risks and requirements. The tests will be prioritized based on the level of risk and priority of requirements, so the high-risk items are tested early in the cycle.

As the IMT system is built on an existing online banking system regression-averse testing strategy will be used to manage the risk of regression where the team will use the automated and manual regression test suite to cover the regression risk.

Product and Project Risks

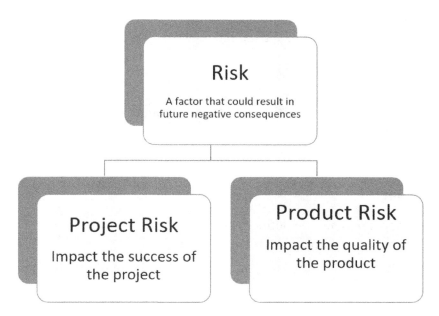

Project and product risk

Product risk involves the possibility that a work product (e.g., a specification, component, system, or test) may fail to satisfy the legitimate needs of its users and/ or stakeholders. Product risks are also called quality risks when they are associated with specific quality characteristics of a product (e.g., functional suitability, reliability, performance efficiency, usability, security, compatibility, maintainability, and portability). Common examples of product risks include:

- The software might not perform its intended functions according to the specification
- The software might not perform its intended functions according to the user, customer, and/or stakeholder needs
- System architecture may not adequately support some non-functional requirement(s)
- A particular computation may be performed incorrectly in some circumstances

Project risk involves the possibility of situations that may have a negative effect on a project's ability to achieve its objectives. Common examples of project risks include:

Project issues:

- Delays may occur in the overall delivery or for individual task completion
- Inaccurate estimates
- Late changes may result in substantial re-work

Organizational issues:

- Project team may not be sufficient or team members not skilled to carry out tasks
- Users, business staff, or subject matter experts may not be available due to conflicting business priorities

Technical issues:

- Requirements may not be defined well enough
- The test environment may not be ready on time

Supplier issues:

- A third party may fail to deliver a necessary product or service on time

Note
Testing reduces product risk, not project risk.

More details on Risk-Based Testing strategy

In Risk-based testing approach testing, preparation and test execution activities are based on the risk associated with the requirements.

This approach requires risk to be assessed based on the following criteria.

Risk Identification and Assessment

The risk will be identified and assessed with the help of relevant stakeholders by selecting the appropriate criterion and values for Business Criticality and Likelihood of failure happening.

Business Criticality -It relates to the potential/expected impact to the business if the function does not work as expected.

Likelihood of failure – It focuses on the likelihood of the failure based on functional and technical complexity.

Risk Prioritisation

Based on the combined Business Criticality and Likelihood of failure, Test Prioritization Matrix is prepared. Each Requirement is then assigned one of the following three values from the matrix.

		Likelihood of Failure		
		3 - Low	2 - Medium	1 - High
Business Criticality	A - High	P1	P1	P1
	B - Medium	P2	P2	P1
	C – Low	P3	P3	P2

Key
P1 – Priority 1
P2 – Priority 2
P3 – Priority 3

Test Prioritization Matrix

E.g. For an online banking system following quality risks, were identified

Risk1: Incorrect yearly interest calculations in reports (a functional risk related to accuracy)

Risk2: Slow response to user input (a non-functional risk related to efficiency and response time)

For **Risk1** the Business Criticality/impact is high as the wrong calculation will impact the whole business and the likelihood is low as it is done once in a year.

For **Risk2** the Business Criticality/impact is low as the user is still able to perform the action but the likelihood is high as with multiple users accessing the system it may happen multiple times in a day.

Once the prioritization is done based on the impact and likelihood then the test team will create appropriate test cases to cover these risks. More tests will be required for high-priority risk items and fewer for the low-priority risk items.

Risk-based testing has the advantage that the most critical areas of the system are tested first. This will minimize the risk even if there are any delays or problems that result in testing being curtailed.

Note
In most organizations, Test Strategy is prepared by Test Manager who is having a good understanding of the overall test approach and testing strategy of the organization. Test Strategy should address how testing will mitigate the risks.

Below is the Test Strategy document prepared for IMT project:

Test Strategy Document

Online Banking IMT Project

Version 1.0

Author: Test Manager

Table of Contents

Document History

Date	Version	Description	Author
12- Jan-YYYY	0.1	The initial version of the document	Test Manager
15- Jan-YYYY	0.2	Inputs from the internal review	Test Manager
18- Jan-YYYY	0.3	Draft distributed for stakeholder review	Test Manager
25- Jan-YYYY	1.0	The final version sent for sign-off	Test Manager

Document Distribution& Sign-off

Name	Title	Responsibility
	Sponsor of the Program	Sign-Off
	Project Manager	Sign-Off
	Business Manager	Sign-off
	Test Lead	Review
	Development Lead	Review
	Team Leader-Support Services	Review
	Senior Developer- IT Production	Review

Note
As the support Services are responsible for building or configuring any new test environments so they need to be informed earlier about any new projects. This will help them scheduling the future work as in big organizations multiple projects run in parallel. IT Production team facilitates the final code deployment to the production environment on the release date and looks after any issues which are found in the production environment. This document is also shared with the senior members of other teams for information purposes; this way they can flag if there are any conflicts with the environment and schedules in advance.

Document Purpose

The purpose of this document is to:

- Clearly define the high-level test strategy to be used for – Online Banking IMT Project
- Provide visibility of the testing strategy early in the project life cycle so that the project team, suppliers and the business have a clear understanding of the proposed testing process and agree to undertake stated activities.
- Define the scope of testing at a high level within each test phase thereby providing a foundation upon which specific test approaches and plans can be documented.
- Outline the intent of the testing effort and allocate responsibilities for the execution of that testing;
- Agree upon the Entry and Exit Criteria for – Online Banking IMT Project

Related Documents

Document
Business Requirements Document (BRD) v1.0
Technical Design Document (TDD) v1.0

1 Introduction

1.1 Project Overview

Currently, the Global Sun customers can't perform International money transfers using the current online banking system. Global Sun is developing a new system to facilitate International Money Transfer via Global Sun Internet Banking. The money is transferred electronically from the customer Global Sun account to the overseas account within 2-3 business days. The customer should be able to send money to over 99 countries around the world using this online IMT system.

According to the IMT solution, the IMT Program will facilitate the following:

- **Fast Electronic Transfer–** The money is transferred electronically from the Global Sun account to the overseas account within 2-3 business days.
- **Real-time market rates-** While transferring via Global Sun Internet Banking customer can see the Real-time market rates for forex and they can take advantage of exchange rate movements during the day and lock in the rate that suits them.

1.2 High-Level System Impacts

The following systems will be impacted to achieve the project's goals and objectives:

System	Functional Impact
Online Banking	Capture the IMT entitlements for the customer.
	Facilitate the account level and daily limits for IMT transfer.
RISK	RISK system feed for Sanctions Risk List (SRL) should be compatible for IMT system

1.3 Assumptions

The following assumptions are identified for IMT Project testing activities:

Assumption	Impact (If Assumption is Incorrect)	Responsible
Stable and usable test environments will be available for IMT Project regression, System and System Integration testing	Start of test phase will not be achievable	Test Lead
All required test data is present in the test environment	Start of test phase will not be achievable	Test Lead

Note
If any of these assumptions are found to be incorrect, it can have a potential impact on the test effort and/or schedule and/or deliverables.

1.4 Project Risks

At the time of the release of this document the following have been identified as risks that could affect the release date.

Risk	Impact	Probability	Mitigation
1010- Testing is not completed on time due to late delivery of code or data/environment issues	High	Low	Extra testing resources from the banking portfolio can be used as a contingency for testing.
1011 – Development team not able to fix the testing defects within defect SLA timeframes	Medium	Medium	Daily defect triage will be happening during the testing phase to check the progress of the defects and resolutions.

Note
The Test Strategy and Test Plan will cover only the project risks which can be migitated by testing team.

1.5 Product Risks

The following have been identified as risks that could affect product quality.

Risk	Impact	Probability	Mitigation
1234 – New IMT functionality can impact the existing functionality of online banking	High	Low	Targeted regression testing of online banking will be done after the system testing of IMT is complete
1235- SWIFT currency rate is not updated in the IMT system	High	High	Extensive Integration testing with the system providing currency rates will be done. Testing will be done to prove that the IMT transfers can't happen if the rates are not updated every 30 mins.
1236-customer can transfer more than their account balance	High	High	Testing will be done to prove that the IMT transfers cannot be performed if the customer is trying to transfer more than their account balance.
1237-customer can transfer money to Sanctions Risk List (SRL) countries	High	Low	Testing will be done to prove that the Sanction list countries are not appearing in the dropdown list for bank locations and beneficiary address country and the list is accessed real-time from the RISK system.

1.6 Constraints

For this project, the following testing constraints are identified:

Constraint	Impact
Test and UAT environments are not connected to the MAIL application test environment.	Email confirmation for the international transfer to the customer's external email id cannot be tested.

Note
These constraints can restrict the scope of testing due to limitations of the test environment or test data. In one of my banking projects, the requirement was to verify that whenever the customer updates their key personal information i.e. address through online banking site the bank will send an email to the customer with the updated changes. In the production environment, the system was connected to a third-party system that was taking care of the email generation. As the test environment was not hooked to the testing environment of that third-party system, there was no way to verify the end to end flow is working. This was highlighted as a testing constraint and the email generation was excluded from the scope of testing. The same is applicable to the IMT project.

1.7 Dependencies

Dependency	Responsible	Impact	By When	Status
None				

Note
Dependencies are applicable when the system needs some input from other systems to start the testing phase, these are mostly applicable for downstream or backend systems.

2   Test Approach

2.1 *Test Phase Definitional and Scope*

The following table defines the test phases and the high-level scope of the test effort for this project.

Phase	Objective	Scope Inclusions	Scope Exclusions
IMT Project Unit Testing	Performed by the Global Sun **development team**. Confirms an individual software component operates as expected. To ensure: All functions work according to program specifications Access to all program logic paths and program module interfaces are working correctly Program edit/validation logic successfully protects the integrity of data elements	Testing of individual IMT specific program code changes.	Testing of system-wide functionality is not performed in the phase.
IMT Project System Test	Performed by the Global Sun **testing team**. The objective of this phase is to confirm that the build meets the Global Sun functional requirement.	Demonstration of IMT Project Functionality Execution of system-level test scripts designed to ensure that the new functionality is present and performs basic operations.	SWIFT interfaces will not be tested.
IMT Project System Integration Test	Performed by the Global Sun **testing team**. • Checks functionality of the integrated system against the design specifications and also original business requirements to ensure: • Functions and end to end business processes work as expected • Fields, screens, data integrity, and calculations match requirements	End to end testing of all the interfaces mentioned in the Technical Design Document IMT (version 1.0)	None

Phase	Objective	Scope Inclusions	Scope Exclusions
IMT Project Regression Test	Performed by the Global Sun **testing team**. A set of tests baselined on existing functionality executed to ensure: • Errors have not been introduced • Customer critical functions still work correctly • Commonly used functions still work correctly • High exposure areas still have integrity	All Critical and High Priority Regression scripts will be executed	Medium and Low Priority Regression scripts will only be executed if time permits.
IMT Project Business Validation (UAT)	A final validation performed by the Business team to ensure a level of comfort prior to implementation. Validation should represent business scenarios performed in end-users day-to-day working life.	End to end business scenarios based on the functional changes implemented with this Release. Validation of high risk and business-critical processes.	Low priority processes and negative scenarios will not be executed during this phase.
IMT Project Production Verification	Confirms new systems functionality is operating correctly in Production. Tests should focus on high risk and business-critical processes.	Functional changes implemented with this Release. Validation of high risk and business-critical processes.	The scope of Production Verification is limited since it is performed in the Production environment. Activities will be limited to those that do not impact customers, accounts or financials.

2.2 Broad Approach by Test Phase

The table below shows the dates and responsible parties for each stage of the testing phases:

Phase	Preparation	Execution	Deliverables
IMT Project System Test	Testing team -3 weeks	Testing team -2 weeks	System Test scripts Status Reports
IMT Project System Integration Test	Testing team – 1 week	Testing team -2 week	SIT Test Scripts Test Status Reports
IMT Project Regression Test	Testing team – 2 days (Existing regression scripts for Online Banking will be used)	Testing team -2 week	Regression Test Scripts Test Status Reports
IMT Project Business Validation	Business Testing Team- 3 days	Business Testing Team- 1 week	Business Validation Test Scripts Test Status Reports
IMT Project Production Verification	Business Testing Team- 2 days	Business Testing Team- 1-2 hrs	PVT Test Scripts

Note
These preparation and execution efforts are based on the initial estimates from the identified risks and draft version of requirements.

2.3 *Test Phase Timelines*

The table below shows the high-level timelines for different testing phases:

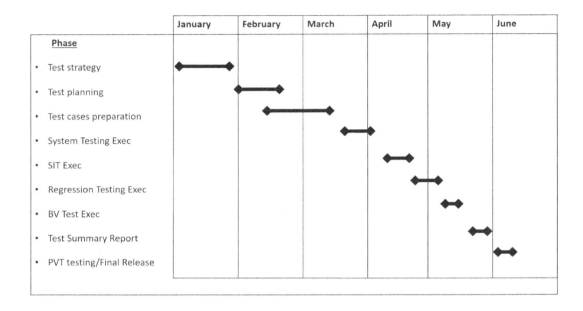

Phase	January	February	March	April	May	June
• Test strategy	◆――◆					
• Test planning		◆――◆				
• Test cases preparation			◆――◆			
• System Testing Exec				◆―◆		
• SIT Exec				◆―◆		
• Regression Testing Exec					◆―◆	
• BV Test Exec					◆◆	
• Test Summary Report					◆◆	
• PVT testing/Final Release						◆◆

3 Test Environment Requirements

3.1 Infrastructure Requirements

Existing online banking environments will be used for this testing effort.

Each environment will interface to the new IMT Service Module.

Online Banking "TEST" environment will be used for:

- System Testing
- System Integration Testing
- Regression Testing

Online Banking "UAT" environment will be used for:

- Business Validation (BV)/UAT Testing

3.2 Software Requirements

Online Banking "TEST" environment will be upgraded with IMT functionality commencing 24th Mar YYYY for IMT Project System and System Integration testing, scheduled to start 01st Apr YYYY.

3.3 Test Data Requirements

Online Banking – Test data has been extracted from Production (dated 10 Jan YYYY) and cut-down and scrambled for use in this Release. The Online Banking Project Team will determine test data requirements that are either identified or created in the Online Banking test environments.

3.4 Test Tools

The testing team, management, and developers require the use of ALM for test planning, scripting, defect management, and reporting.

Unified Functional Testing (UFT) tool will be used to run automated regression tests.

3.5 Infrastructure/Environment Control

- Online Banking Project team will manage the test environment with regards to execution and software control
- The development team will migrate the code to the test and UAT environment
- The Production Support team will migrate the code to the production environment

4 Test Phase Entry and Exit Criteria (Stage Containment)

Moving from one test phase to the next will consist of meeting the relevant entry and exit criteria. Below is a list of the entry/exit specific to this project.

Phase	Entry Criteria	Exit Criteria
IMT Project Unit Test	Not required	Unit Testing is deemed complete when the following exit criteria are met: • The build is complete. • Unit and Integration Testing are complete. • All Severity 1 & 2 defects found have been fixed.
IMT Project System Test	Build is complete and successfully deployed to System Test environment	ST Testing is deemed complete when the following exit criteria are met: • All high priority test scripts have been executed. • No Severity 1 & 2 defects are outstanding. • No Severity 3 & 4 defects are outstanding (unless agreed by the Management Committee)
IMT Project System Integration Test	The following entry criteria must be met before the commencement of System Integration Testing (SIT): • Connectivity test to SWIFT Service works • System Test exit criteria have been met.	SIT Testing is deemed complete when the following exit criteria are met: • All high priority test scripts have been executed. • Acceptable levels (as determined by the Management Committee) of medium and low priority test scripts have been executed. • No Severity 1 & 2 defects are outstanding. • No Severity 3 & 4 defects are outstanding (unless agreed by the Management Committee)

Phase	Entry Criteria	Exit Criteria
IMT Project Regression Test	The following entry criteria must be met before the commencement of IMT Project Regression Testing: • System and System Integration Test (SIT) Test exit criteria have been met	IMT Project Regression Testing is deemed complete when the following exit criteria are met: • All Critical and High Priority Regression test scripts have been executed. • Acceptable levels (as determined by the Management Committee) of medium and low priority Regression test scripts have been executed. • No Severity 1 & 2 defects are outstanding. • No Severity 3 & 4 defects are outstanding (unless agreed by the Management Committee)
IMT Project Business Validation	The following entry criteria must be met before commencement Business Validation (BV). • System, System Integration Test (SIT) and Regression Test exit criteria have been met. • BV Planning and Preparation is complete. • The BV environment is ready and accessible. • Systems access for all business personnel has been established. • Appropriate test data is available in the UAT environment	• Business Validation (BV) is deemed complete when the following exit criteria are met: • All high priority BV test scripts have been executed. • Acceptable levels (as determined by the Management Committee) of medium and low priority BV test scripts have been executed. • No Severity 1 & 2 defects are outstanding. • No Severity 3 & 4 defects are outstanding (unless agreed by the Management Committee)
IMT Project Production Verification	BV Testing has been completed and Signoff Received Known defects have been documented	PVT has been performed and the results have been signed off (Go / No-Go Meeting)

4.1 Defect Management

The IMT Test Lead is the first point of contact for all defects. A defect can take the form of a software error, infrastructure setup error, test script error or data error, however, the same reporting and tracking process applies to all defects detected as part of – Online Banking IMT project.

4.2 Defect Logging

ALM (Application Lifecycle Management) tool will be used to log defects. All project team members will be provided access to ALM so that they can log and/or access defects. The Test Lead will facilitate an initial "triage" activity with nominated Business resources whereby all defects are evaluated and assessed for completeness/ validity.

4.3 Defect Severity & SLA

Severity	Description	Fix time	Description of Severity
1	Critical	½ business day	Showstopper.
			The system cannot run or perform a major function. The testing of subsequent functions cannot be performed. Fixing the problem is critical for the acceptance of the system.
			Testing cannot continue, or the majority of test scripts would be invalidated if testing continued.
2	Major	2 business day	A major function provides incorrect information or cannot be assessed. A minor function provides an incorrect result and no suitable workaround exists.
			Testing can continue. Testing of impaired function and related function is impacted.
3	Minor	3 business day	Low priority problems. Minor functions that provide an incorrect result should be resolved, but a workaround exists.
			Testing can continue. May invalidate a localized group of test scripts/steps.
4	Low	5 business day	Cosmetic or similar errors that do not impact the functionality or performance of the system but should be resolved.
			All testing can continue. Only test scripts specifically testing the problem affected.

4.4 Defect Resolution Meetings

The defect resolution process often requires close contact (and action) between testers, business resources, project manager and development teams. During the test execution, daily defect resolution meetings (defect triage) will be held to discuss/ determine the following:

- All open defects in severity order.
- The priority of fix and validity.

4.5 Defect Tracking and Reporting

Progress will be reported via the standard Test Status Reporting template daily.

-----------------------End of the Test Strategy document-----------------------

16 | Test Estimation

The effort for each testing task needs to be calculated so they can be aligned into the project plan. This applies to both test preparation and test execution activities. With proper test estimation, we can get an approximate target for costs and completion dates associated with the testing activities for a particular project. The best test estimates should:

- Provide specific, detailed catalogs of the costs, resources, tasks, and people involved
- Present, for each activity estimated, the most likely cost, effort, and duration
- Represent the collective wisdom of experienced practitioners and have the support of the participants involved

There are two main approaches for test estimation:

Metrics based approach: In this approach, the estimation of testing effort is done based on the historical data which is collected from the previous releases for the same project or data from similar projects within the organization or the industry.

For example, the testing team has collected the following metrics from the previous releases for test case preparation:

<u>Release 1:</u>

Requirement Type	Number of Requirements	The corresponding number of test cases created
Complex	10	41
Medium	20	62
Low	40	89

Note
The requirement is a high-level description of the functionality for the system under development.

Release 2:

Requirement Type	Number of Requirements	The corresponding number of test cases created
Complex	5	22
Medium	12	38
Low	30	61

Release 3:

Requirement Type	Number of Requirements	The corresponding number of test cases created
Complex	8	30
Medium	4	11
Low	10	22

Now for **Release 4** if we have to estimate the average test cases required to test a complex requirement. We can use the historical data as below:

Number of test cases required for each complex requirement

$$= \frac{41/10 + 22/5 + 30/8}{3} = 4.0833$$

Where 3 is the number of releases for which we have data. In this case, we can say that for each complex requirement we require around four test cases. Now if we know the time required for test preparation for one test case we can calculate the total effort for a complex requirement.

As the historical data increases the accuracy of the estimation will improve.

Expert-based Approach: In this approach, the estimation of the test effort is done based on input from the task owner or the person who will be carrying out the relevant testing tasks or by experts in that area. In this context 'experts' could be:

- Business experts
- Technical experts
- Test architects
- Test consultants
- Developers
- Technical architects
- Technical designers

There are many ways that this approach could be used. Here are two examples:

- Ask the task owners to get the estimate of their task in isolation. Amalgamate the individual estimates when received; build in any required contingency, to arrive at the estimate.
- Distribute to known experts who develop their individual view of the overall estimate and then discuss together to agree on and/or debate the estimate that will go forward.

The best practice is to combine both the techniques to get the best estimates. In most organizations, initial estimate is taken based on the historical data and then this data is validated with experts (mostly in the group meetings) to arrive on an accurate estimate. A buffer is taken which considers all factors that can influence the cost, effort, and duration of the testing activities. Some of the factors can be:

- Skills of the testing team. If the testers are new that may increase the effort.
- Size of the project and complexity of the domain.
- The testing strategy used in the project

Examples of estimation techniques in sequential software development:

- **Defect removal models** are examples of the **metrics-based approach**, where volumes of defects and time to remove them are captured and reported, which then provides a basis for estimating future projects of a similar nature.
- **Wideband Delphi estimation technique** is an example of the **expert-based approach** in which a group of experts provides estimates based on their experience.

Wideband Delphi estimation method

In most of the projects for expert base estimation, the **Wideband Delphi** estimation method is used which is a consensus-based technique for estimating effort. Following key points are taken into account when using this technique:

- **Experts selection**

This includes selecting experts based on their expertise in the activity under-estimation, required knowledge domain, and complexity involved in the project. The experts can be part of the project team or from outside the project.

- **Providing relevant information to the Experts**

Once the experts are selected, they are given information about the objectives of the estimation, the scope of the activity and project, project complexity, estimated deadline and expected deliverables from the experts. Based on this information, the experts prepare their schedules and devise a plan to carry out the estimation activity.

- **Gather estimates from the Experts**

Based on the information provided, the experts will provide their effort for the tasks.

Expert Name	Effort
Expert 1	X
Expert 2	Y
Expert 3	Z

- **Deciding the final estimates**

These estimates can be combined to arrive at the final estimates. Based on high and low estimates, an average estimate can be drawn. Sometimes low and high estimates are discussed with all the experts in a meeting to arrive on the final estimate.

Note
For the IMT project, the initial test estimate was done based on the historical data from the online banking project. After that, the Test Manager has organized a meeting with the team to review and validate this to arrive at a final estimate. A buffer was added to this final estimate based on the identified risks, the complexity of the project, and the skills/experience of the testing team.

17 Test Plan

The test plan provides details on how the testing team will implement the Test Strategy (i.e. the test approach). It also defines **who is responsible for the tasks** and the **timelines** for each test level. The Test Plan like Test Strategy is a living document that means it is continually edited and updated during the project based on any new identified risks and/or any other changes to project requirements or schedule.

The test plan covers all the testing work to be done on a particular project, including the particular levels to be carried out, the relationships among those levels, and between test levels and corresponding development activities. The test plan should discuss in detail how the testing team will implement the **risk mitigation approach** defined in the test strategy. The test plan should be consistent with the organization test policy and the project test strategy, and, in specific areas where it is not, should explain those deviations and exceptions, including any potential impact resulting from the deviations. It also describes the activities to be carried out within each test level providing schedule, task, and milestone details.

Below is the Test plan document prepared for IMT project:

Test Plan

Online Banking IMT Project

(Functional Test Plan Covering the Phases ST, SIT, Regression, and BV)

Author: Test Lead

Version: 1.0

Table of Contents

Document History

Date	Version	Description	Author
27 Jan. YYYY	0.1	Initial Draft	Test Lead
12 Feb YYYY	0.2	Input from the internal review	Test Lead
18 Feb YYYY	1.0	Input from external review	Test Lead

Document Distribution

Name	Title	Responsibility
	Sponsor of the Program	Sign-Off
	Project Manager	Sign-Off
	Test Manager	Sign-Off
	Business Manager	Sign-off
	Development Lead	Review
	Team Leader-Support Services	Review
	Senior Developer- IT Production	Review
	Testing Team members	Review

1 Introduction

Currently, the Global Sun customers must visit bank branches to do International money transfer which involves using the physical paper form and is a tedious and time-consuming activity. Most of the Global Sun competitors are having online banking. Global Sun is developing a new system, so the customers can make an International Money Transfer via Global Sun Internet. The money is transferred electronically from the Global Sun account to the overseas account within 2-3 business days. The customer should be able to send money to over 99 countries around the world using the online IMT system.

According to the IMT proposal, the IMT Program will facilitate the following:

- **Fast Electronic Transfer–** The money is transferred electronically from the Global Sun account to the overseas account within 2-3 business days.

- **Real-time market rates-** While transferring via Global Sun Internet Banking customers can see the Real-time market rates for forex and they can take advantage of exchange rate movements during the day and lock in the rate that suits them.

1.1 Document Purpose

This document is intended for:

- All project stakeholders to agree upon the Entry and Exit Criteria of ST, SIT, Regression & BV Test Phases for Online Banking Release IMT Project

- Establish the test deliverables required for Online Banking Release IMT Project

- Identify and seek to mitigate risks, assumptions, constraints, and dependencies that could negatively impact the test effort

- Business Stakeholders to agree to make the required testing resources available at the required times within the testing schedule for BV testing

- Project team members involved in the test effort to understand their roles and responsibilities; and

- IT Production to enable the setup of the required test environment(s)

1.2 Related Documents

Test cases
Regression Test scripts for IMT Project v2.1 (ALM location)

Note
Regression testing & regression test scenarios are covered in detail in chapter 25- Regression Testing

1.3 Assumptions

The following assumptions have been made during the creation of this document:

Assumption	Impact (If Assumption is Incorrect)	Responsible	Confirmed by date
The TEST environment is available for the new upgrade (IMT Project) from 23rd MAR YYYY.	Start of test phase will not be achievable	IMT Test Lead	15 Mar YYYY
All required test data is present in the test environment	Start of test phase will not be achievable	IMT Test Lead	19 Mar YYYY

2 Overview of Test Scope

2.1 Test Objectives

The primary objectives of testing are to validate:

- New IMT functionality is working as per the specifications
- The business functionality of Online Banking is working as per the previous release R2.2

2.2 Test Scope Inclusions

- Testing of all the test scenarios created as part of IMT testing
- Selected test cases from the Online banking Regression Test suite will be executed to make sure the new IMT functionality has not impacted the existing online banking functionality

2.3 Test Scope Exclusions

The following functionality is out of scope for IMT Project Release:

- Email confirmation for the international transfer payment to the customer's external email id.

Note
Test scope exclusions are to highlight to all stakeholder any area which is not part of testing. The global sun testing environment is not connected to the email server therefore we cannot verify that after the transfer is successful the email is sent to the customer's external email id. The scope is to only check that the message is there in the online banking mailbox.

2.4 Test Deliverables

The major deliverables to be supplied by the Test Team in support of the test activity are:

- Test Plan (this document)
- Test Scenarios (High-level test cases)
- Test Cases (for manual test execution will be stored in ALM tool)
- Test Results and evidence (will be recorded in ALM tool)
- Test Status Reports
- Test Summary Report

2.5 Testing Milestones

Following is an outline of key Testing Milestones for Online Banking Release IMT Project testing

Test Stage	Milestone	Responsibility	Start Date	End Date
Test Planning	Test plan signoff	Test Manager	27th Jan YYYY	18th Feb YYYY
Test Preparation	Completion of Test Scripts	Test Lead	15th Feb YYYY	17th Mar YYYY
Test Execution	Availability of Test Environment / Delivery of Build	Test Lead	24th Mar YYYY	30th Mar YYYY
	Smoke Testing for the Online Banking Release IMT Project	Test Lead	1st Apr YYYY	1st Apr YYYY
	ST Testing for Online Banking Release IMT Project	Test Lead	2nd Apr YYYY	15th Apr YYYY
	SIT Testing for Online Banking Release IMT Project	Test Lead	16th Apr YYYY	27th Apr YYYY
	Regression Testing	Test Lead	28th Apr YYYY	11th May YYYY
	BV Testing	Business Manager	13th May YYYY	19th May YYYY
Test Closure	Completion of the Test Summary Report	Test Lead	20th May YYYY	28th May YYYY
Test Closure	Test Summary Report signoff during the formal walkthrough.	Test Manager	29th May YYYY	29th May YYYY

2.6 Constraints

The international transfer email confirmation to the customer's external email id cannot be tested.

2.7 Dependencies

Dependency	Responsible	Impact	By When	Status
Testing for this Release is dependent on the successful build of existing Online Banking system from production in the TEST environment	Test Lead	Testing will not be able to start.	20 Mar YYYY	In Progress

2.8 Project Risks

At the time of the initial release of this document the following have been identified as risks that could affect the release date. These risks are also recorded in the Project Risk Register.

Risk	Impact	Probability	Mitigation
1010- Testing is not completed on time due to late delivery or data/ environment issues	High	Low	Extra testing resources from the banking portfolio can be used as a contingency for testing.
1011 – Development team may not able to fix the testing defects within SLA timeframes	Medium	Medium	Daily defect triage will be happening during the testing phase to check the progress of the defects and resolutions.

2.9 Product Risks

The following have been identified as risks that could affect product quality.

Risk	Impact	Probability	Mitigation
1234 – New IMT functionality can impact the existing functionality of online banking	High	Low	Targeted regression testing of online banking will be done after the system testing of IMT is complete
1235- SWIFT currency rate is not updated in the IMT system	High	High	Extensive Integration testing with the system providing currency rates will be done. Testing will be done to prove that the IMT transfers can't happen if the rates are not updated every 30 mins.
1236-customer can transfer more than their account balance	High	High	Testing will be done to prove that the IMT transfers can't happen if the customer is trying to transfer more than their account balance.
1237-Customer can transfer money to Sanctions Risk list (SRL) countries	High	Low	Testing will be done to prove that the Sanction list countries are not appearing in the dropdown list for bank locations and beneficiary address country and the list is accessed real-time from the RISK system.

Note
During the course of project execution if any new product risk or project risk are identified the document needs to be updated to reflect them.

3 Test Approach

The test approach described below is in adherence with the Global Sun Bank Test Methodology

3.1 Test Planning and Control

This test plan defines the plan and approach for conducting this testing effort. The test scope, milestone dates, risks, dependencies and resource requirements defined in this test plan will be closely monitored frequently throughout the entire test effort using the following control mechanisms:

Test Planning Component	Control Mechanism	Comment
Milestones	Test Schedule	Daily tracking against planned test effort.
Resources	Work Effort	Daily tracking of work completed against planned work effort.
Issues & Risks	Issues & Risk register	All issues and risks defined in this test plan and ongoing throughout the testing effort will be entered into the Issues & Risk database. Issue resolutions and risk mitigations will be monitored.
Unscheduled Outages	Downtime Register	A downtime register will be established to record impact to unscheduled outages throughout the test effort (primarily during test execution). All outages will be assessed for impact on milestones.
Communication	Daily Status Report	Tracking against work effort, issues, risks, and defects will be reported daily to key project stakeholders.

3.2 Test Preparation

- For the new IMT functionality, the IMT testing team will create the test cases.
- For the targeted regression testing, already existing regression test cases will be used.
- The available Automated test scripts will be used for regression testing.
- Test Environment will be upgraded to new IMT functionality on date 20-Mar-YYYY.
- The system, system integration testing, and targeted regression testing will be performed after the upgrade.

3.3 *Regression Test Coverage Determination*

The development team will provide release notes which are further discussed with the Development team, based on the discussion analysis is done by the testing team and the coverage of targeted regression is determined.

Note
More details on Regression test coverage is in chapter 25- Regression Testing

3.4 *Test Execution*

- Targeted Regression Test scripts will be executed to verify the existing Online Banking functionality.
- Automation scripts will be used for some of the targeted regression tests.
- Defects will be logged in the ALM under Release IMT Project.
- Daily Test Defect Reports and Test Status reports will be collated and distributed to project stakeholders.

3.5 *Resource Requirements*

SIT and targeted regression testing will be done by the current testing team.

For the BV test preparation and execution, 2 testers will be required from the business team for 2 weeks.

3.6 *Test Metrics*

The following agreed metrics would be obtained and reported on during test execution:

No	Test Metrics
1	Total number of defects by test phase (accumulative total)
2	Total number of defects by severity and/or status
3	Total number of outstanding defects (not closed) by severity and/or status
4	Test Progress (Test Scripts executed vs. Test Scripts outstanding)
5	Test Status (Test Scripts passed vs. Test Scripts failed vs. Test Scripts not completed).

3.7 Software Gate closed

3.7.1 Gate Closed

As per current milestones, the gate closed date is 2 weeks after the System testing starts.

By definition, Gate Closed has the following impacts:

- Only migrations for defect fixes linked to a project will be allowed to test environments.

Note
The later changes to the software can have an impact on the already tested code. After Gate Closed no major changes are allowed and only defect fixes will be done. After Gate locked only changes related to the fix of Severity 1 and 2 defects are allowed after an assessment of impacted areas. The gate closed and Gate Locked ensures that the build which is tested by the testing team is not having any major changes after the majority of testing is completed.

3.7.2 Gate Locked

Gate Locked is scheduled to commence 2 weeks after the Gate closed schedule.

Gate Locked has the following impacts:

- All software migration requests are to be referred to the Project Manager for authorization prior to migrating to the Release test environments.
- Any Severity 3 or 4 defects may not be approved for migration in this period

3.8 Test Closure

Upon completion of the testing effort, a Test Summary Report will be completed and distributed for formal signoff by Project Stakeholders and the Business Sponsor. A formal review meeting will be initiated to walkthrough test results on date 29-May-YYYY. The outcome of the meeting will depend upon the number of open severity 1 and severity 2 defects raised during testing.

3.9   Entry Criteria

The following entry criteria must be met prior to the commencement of Release IMT Project Testing:

- IMT Project build is complete and deployed to the test environment
- The TEST environment required for testing IMT functionality has been set up.
- System access for all testers has been established.
- Appropriate test data is available in the TEST environment
- Initial verification of build completed (smoke testing).

Note
The smoke test is an initial test to make sure that the software under test is ready for testing. More details about smoke testing in chapter 23.

3.10   Exit / Acceptance Criteria

Testing will not be deemed complete unless all of the following exit criteria are met for each test level:

- All test scripts planned for testing executed.
- All retest of defects completed
- No Severity 1 defects are open.
- No Severity 2 defects are open.
- All Severity 3 defects agreed by business stakeholders. Any impact on Business has been reviewed and an acceptable workaround has been documented and agreed.
- All business workarounds for the severity 4 defects accepted.

3.11 Defect Management

3.11.1 Daily Defect Reviews

New defects will be reviewed daily with the Development and Business team during defect resolution meetings (defect triage) to determine:

- The validity of the defect.
- The severity of the defect.
- Whether the defect needs to be resolved now or can be deferred for later release.

3.11.2 Defect Severities & SLA

Severity	Description	Fix time	Description of Severity
1	Critical	½ business day	Showstopper. The system cannot run or perform a major function. The testing of subsequent functions cannot be performed. Fixing the problem is critical for the acceptance of the system. Testing cannot continue, or the majority of test scripts would be invalidated if testing continued.
2	Major	2 business day	A major function provides incorrect information or cannot be assessed. A minor function provides an incorrect result and no suitable workaround exists. Testing can continue. Testing of impaired function and related function is impacted.
3	Minor	3 business day	Low priority problems. Minor functions that provide an incorrect result should be resolved, but a workaround exists. Testing can continue. May invalidate a localized group of test scripts/steps.
4	Low	5 business day	Cosmetic or similar errors that do not impact the functionality or performance of the system but should be resolved. All testing can continue. Only test scripts specifically testing the problem affected.

3.11.3 Defect Workflow

All defects will be logged and tracked through ALM.

The diagram below describes the workflow for defects:

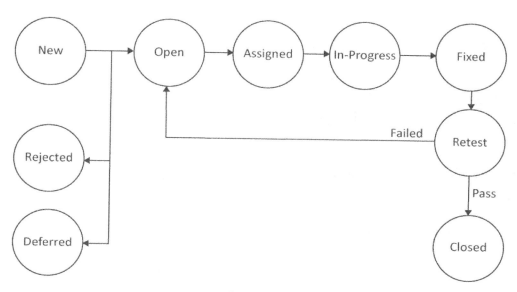

Defect Life Cycle

4 Test Environment Requirements

4.1 Infrastructure Requirements

TEST environment will be used for release IMT Project ST, SIT, and regression testing & UAT environment will be used for BV testing.

4.2 Software Requirements

Online Banking "TEST" environment will be upgraded with IMT functionality commencing 24th Mar YYYY for IMT Project System and System Integration testing, scheduled to start 01st Apr YYYY.

4.3 Test Data Requirements

Online Banking – Test data has been extracted from Production (dated 10th Jan YYYY) and cut-down and scrambled for use in this Release.

----------------------End of TEST PLAN DOCUMENT----------------------

18 Functional Requirements

Functional requirements are generally covered in Business Requirement Document (BRD). In some organizations, it is called the Functional Specification Document (FSD) or Functional Requirements Specification (FRS). These documents are generally prepared by the business analyst's working on the project. This document covers the following sections in detail:

- Problem statement
- Business objective
- Customer needs and insights
- Key features
- In scope
- Out of scope
- Functional requirements
- Risks
- Issues
- Assumptions
- Constrains
- Dependencies

For the testing team, the **Functional Requirements** section is important as it helps testers to understand the requirements, so later they can create the test cases based on that. The draft version of the BRD is generally ready before the Test plan so the Test Lead/Manager can estimate the testing activities based on that.

Following are the high-level **Functional Requirements** for International Money Transfer (IMT):

#	Area	Requirement Description	Criticality 1: Essential 2: Important 3: Desirable
R1.1	**Enable the IMT menu**	Enable a new menu item "**New international transfer**" under **Fund transfer** for online banking users authorized for International transfers.	1
R1.2		After the user selects the new menu item "**New international transfer**" they should be transferred to the "New international transfer" main page.	1
R2.1		User account details should be auto-populated with the customer name and accounts eligible for International transfers.	1
R2.2		The user should be allowed to select the from account used for the transfer from the list. This list should only display checking accounts as they are only eligible for International transfers.	1
R2.3		There should be a **Beneficiary's bank location** field which should show only the valid list of countries for the bank location, the countries which are part of the Sanctions Risk List (SRL) should not show up in the list. IMT system should access the Sanctions Risk List (SRL) from the RISK system in real-time.	1
R2.4		User should be able to select a location from the Beneficiary's bank location	1
R2.5	**New international transfer main screen**	Under **the Beneficiary's bank details** there should be an option for the user to enter an account number of maximum 12 digits or a valid IBAN.	1
R2.6		Under **the Beneficiary's bank details** there should be an option for the user to enter a Bank SWIFT/BIC code. A valid SWIFT/BIC code should have: • first 4-letter as bank code • then 2-letter for country code • then 2-letter or number location code • followed by 3-letter or number for branch code (optional)	1
R2.7		Under the **Beneficiary's details,** there should be an option for the user to enter the beneficiary's name which can be a maximum of 25 characters.	1
R2.8		Under the Beneficiary's details, there should be a list of all countries for the user address, the countries which are part of the Sanctions Risk list (SRL) should not show up in the list. IMT system should access the Sanctions Risk list (SRL) from the RISK system in real-time.	1
R2.9		Users should be able to select a country for the beneficiary address from the country's dropdown.	1

#	Area	Requirement Description	Criticality 1: Essential 2: Important 3: Desirable
R2.10		Under **the Beneficiary's details,** there should be an option for the user to enter primary address information which can be a maximum of 25 alphanumeric characters.	1
R2.11		Under **the Beneficiary's details,** there should be an option for the user to enter secondary address information which can be a maximum of 25 alphanumeric characters.	2
R2.12		Under **the Beneficiary's details,** there should be an option for the user to enter a message for the beneficiary which can be a maximum of 40 alphanumeric characters.	3
R2.13		Under **Beneficiary's details** should have an option for the user to enter a description of transfer which can be a maximum of 20 alphanumeric characters.	3
R2.14		After the user has input the mandatory fields on the page, they should have an option to proceed to the next screen.	1
R3.1	**Transfer main screen error handling**	If the user entered account number and IBAN are invalid in the Transfer main screen and the user tries to proceed to the next screen • Highlight the field with an exclamation sign • Display error message in red "Account number or IBAN is invalid. Please try again. " • User stays on the **"New international transfer"** screen	1
R3.2		If the user entered SWIFT code is invalid in the Transfer main screen and the user tries to proceed to the next screen • Highlight the field with an exclamation sign • Display the error message in red "SWIFT code is invalid. Please try again. " • User stays on the **"New international transfer"** main screen	1

#	Area	Requirement Description	Criticality 1: Essential 2: Important 3: Desirable
R4.1		Under **Transfer details,** there should be an option for the user to enter the amount which can be greater than or equal to 10 and less than and equal to the daily IMT limit set by the bank (check the daily IMT limit in RISK system the current limit is AUD 10,000)	1
R4.2		Under **Transfer details,** the standard international fee should be auto-populated after the user enter the amount (check the RISK system for standard fees). This should be a non-editable field.	1
R4.3		Under **Transfer details,** the user should be displayed the total cost after they enter the amount. • It should be the sum of the amount and the standard international fee if the user has selected the option to pay the fees from the account. • It should be equal to the amount field if the user has selected the option to pay the fees from the Funds they are sending. This should be auto-populated and should be a non-editable field.	2
R4.4		The current exchange rate for the beneficiary currency from SWIFT should be displayed as the current rate for the user. This should be a non-editable field.	1
R4.5	**Transfer Detail Screen**	The current date time when the exchange rate is retrieved from SWIFT should be displayed for the user. This should be a non-editable field.	1
R4.6		The user should be displayed the auto-populated what beneficiary will receive which should be the (total cost x current rate) This should be a non-editable field.	2
R4.7		Under **Transfer details,** the user should be provided an option to select whether the fees should be deducted from the total amount or as an extra from the sending account	2
R4.8		Under **Transfer details,** the user should be provided an option to view the terms and conditions for international money transfer	1
R4.9		International transfer terms and conditions should be the same as the terms and conditions defined in the RISK system. Latest terms and conditions in Appendix A (After the requirements)	1
R4.10		There should be an option for the user to acknowledge that they have read and agreed to the terms and conditions	1
R4.11		There should be an option for the user to go back and change the details on the previous screen. All previous pages should retain the values entered previously.	1
R4.12		After the user has input the valid amount and acknowledged the terms and conditions, they should have an option to proceed to the next screen	1

#	Area	Requirement Description	Criticality 1: Essential 2: Important 3: Desirable
R5.1	**Transfer Details screen error handling**	If the user entered amount is less than 10 (minimum limit in RISK system) and the user tries to proceed to the next screen • Highlight the field with an exclamation sign • Display error message "Amount less than the minimum limit. Please try again." in red text • User stays on the **"New international transfer detail"** screen	1
R5.2		If the Total cost is greater than the account balance and the user tries to proceed to the next screen • Highlight the field with an exclamation sign • Display error message "Amount greater than the Account balance. Please try again." in red text • User stays on the **"New international transfer detail"** screen	1
R5.3		If the user entered amount is greater than the IMT limit in RISK system (current limit AUD 10,000) and the user tries to proceed to the next screen • Highlight the field with an exclamation sign • Display error message "Amount greater than the maximum limit. Please try again." in red text • User stays on the **"New international transfer detail"** screen	1
R5.4		If the user has not entered the amount and the user tries to proceed to the next screen • Highlight the field with an exclamation sign • Display error message "Please enter the amount and try again." in red text • User stays on the **"New international transfer detail"** screen	1
R5.5		When the user tries to proceed to the next screen and the user has not acknowledged the terms and conditions • Highlight the field with an exclamation sign • Display error message "Please acknowledge terms and conditions." in red text • User stays on the **"New international transfer detail"** screen	1

#	Area	Requirement Description	Criticality 1: Essential 2: Important 3: Desirable
R6.1	Transfer confirmation screen	Under **view and confirm your transfer** the user should be able to view the amount which should be same as the Total amount from in the **transfer detail screen** which is non-editable	1
R6.2		Under **view and confirm your transfer** the user should be able to view the **from account** selected in the **transfer main screen** for payment which is non-editable	1
R6.3		Under **view and confirm your transfer** the user should be able to view the **beneficiary account** entered in the **transfer detail screen** which is non-editable	1
R6.4		Under **view and confirm your transfer** the user should be displayed the payment date which should be the To-day Date + 2-3 business Days non-editable (Weekend and public holidays are considered as non-business days)	2
R6.5		Following disclaimer should be displayed to the user after the payment date: "It takes 2-3 business days to process international transfers Important: Please check that the account details are correct. We may not be able to recover funds sent to the wrong account."	1
R6.6		There should be an option for the user to go back and change the details on the previous screen. All previous pages should retain the values entered previously.	2
R6.7		The user should be provided with an option to confirm the payment and proceed to the next screen.	1
R7.1	Transfer Receipt screen	On the **Receipt page**, the user should be displayed the following fields based on the selection and entry from the previous screens • Amount • Updated balance • From • To • Payment date All the above fields should be non-editable.	2
R7.2		The user should be provided a receipt number which is a unique 12-digit alphanumeric value auto-generated by the system	2
R7.3		The user should be provided an option to print the confirmation details.	3
R7.4		The confirmation details should be provided to the user as a new mail in the internet banking mailbox and their external email id provided to the bank.	3

Appendix A: International transfer terms and conditions

1. Foreign currency rate

2. The foreign currency rates available to the applicant depend on the value of the international transfer and are subject to change or withdrawal at any time without

1.2 If the international transfer referred to in the applicant's international transfer instruction is to be made in the same currency as the currency of the source account, GS will debit the source account with the amount of the international transfer referred to in the applicant's international transfer instruction; or in a currency different to the currency of the source account, GS will debit the source account with an amount that is equal to the transfer currency amount referred to in the applicants international transfer instruction after applying the relevant currency exchange rate determined by GS.

The relevant currency exchange rate will be: 1.Where an international transfer is to be made on the day of the applicant's international transfer instruction, GS will apply the exchange rate set out in the "Your receipt record" screen.

The GS selling rate applicable at the time of conversion may differ from the exchange rate at the time that the applicant made the payment instruction. Where the GS selling rate is used in relation to an international transfer, details of the actual rate applied by GS will generally be available within the service once the international payment instruction is processed by GS.

1.3 Other financial service providers involved in connection with the processing of an international transfer instruction may perform further currency conversions to facilitate the processing of that instruction without reference to the beneficiary of the international transfer, the applicant or GS.

3. Foreign currency transactions can involve the risk of loss because of movement in exchange rates or interest rates. It is important that the applicant understands these risks before entering into a foreign currency transaction and understands that any loss will be passed on to and will be payable by the applicant.

4. In the event an international transfer is returned by an overseas financial institution, GS will credit the source account with the Australian dollar equivalent of the amount received, at the currency exchange rate determined by GS in accordance with 1.2 in connection with the applicant's international payment instruction, less any fees levied by overseas banks in connection with failed transactions.

5. Fees

2.1 GS will charge you a fee to process your international payment. This fee is $2.99 per transaction when you make your international money transfer via the service in a foreign currency and $3.5 per transaction when you make your international money transfer via the service in Australian Dollars. This fee is payable in accordance with the service terms and conditions applicable to all fees payable in connection with use of the service. For more information about fees and charges, please refer to A guide to Fees & Charges (Personal banking fees), and Business Banking Fees (A guide to fees and charges), whichever is relevant to you.

6. The majority of overseas banks levy processing charges which vary between banks and countries. GS will pay these costs and will instruct overseas banks to charge these costs to GS. However, in some instances beyond GS's control, this may not be possible, and overseas banks may deduct their costs from the money you send, which will result in the beneficiary receiving a lesser amount than expected.

7. Liability

The liabilities set out in these terms and conditions are in addition to the liability provisions set out in the service terms and conditions as they apply to use of the service and the provision of an instruction in connection with the service. To remove any doubt where the applicant is engaged in a personal EFT transaction the provisions in the service terms and conditions applicable to personal EFT transactions prevail.

Note
In most of the projects, after the BRD is ready the business analyst will organize a requirement walk-through session with the project team. It is the responsibility of the testers to ask relevant questions to clarify all their doubts and assumptions regarding the requirements during this session. The requirements should be crystal clear to the testers before they start working on the test cases. They should not make any assumptions about the requirements while writing the test cases.

Note
Static Testing - As soon as the draft version of the requirement document is ready static testing can be performed using reviews to find any inconsistencies, ambiguities, contradictions, omissions, inaccuracies, and redundancies in the requirements. In most of the projects, a formal process is followed where the review sessions are planned and a moderator effectively runs these sessions, defects are documented and tracked using a defect management system.

19 High-Level Test Case

Once the first draft of requirements is ready the testing team will start analyzing the requirements to create the high-level test cases. These high-level test cases are then mapped back to the requirements and given a priority based on the business criticality of the requirements. The sample high-level test cases for IMT project are shown below:

#	Requirement Description	Test case #	Test case Name	High-level test cases
R1.1	Enable a new menu item "**New international transfer**" under **Fund transfer** for online banking users authorized for International transfers.	TC_01	Verify IMT Menu_1	To verify user entitled for International transfer can see the 'New International Transfer' menu item
		TC_02	Verify IMT Menu_2	To verify user not entitled for International transfer cannot see the 'New International Transfer' menu item
R1.2	After the user selects the new menu item "**New international transfer**" they should be transferred to the "New international transfer" main page.	TC_03	Verify IMT Menu_3	To verify the user is navigated to 'New International Transfer' main screen
R2.1	User account details should be auto-populated with the customer name and accounts eligible for International transfers.	TC_04	Verify IMT Main Screen_1	To verify user accounts are populated on 'New International Transfer' main screen
R2.2	The user should be allowed to select the from account used for the transfer from the list. This list should only display checking accounts as they are only eligible for International transfers.	TC_05	Verify IMT Main Screen_2	To verify the user can select the eligible account from the account list for the International transfer

#	Requirement Description	Test case #	Test case Name	High-level test cases
R2.3	There should be a **Beneficiary's bank location** field which should show only the valid list of countries for the bank location, the countries which are part of the Sanctions Risk list (SRL) should not show up in the list. IMT system should access the Sanctions Risk list (SRL) from the RISK system in real-time.	TC_06	Verify IMT Main Screen_3	To verify only the eligible country for transfers are displayed in the beneficiary bank location dropdown
R2.4	User should be able to select a location from the Beneficiary's bank location	TC_07	Verify IMT Main Screen_4	To verify the user can select a country from the beneficiary bank location dropdown
R2.5	Under **the Beneficiary's bank details** there should be an option for the user to enter an account number of maximum 12 digits or a valid IBAN.	TC_08	Verify IMT Main Screen_5	To verify the user can only enter a valid account number or IBAN in beneficiary bank details
R2.6	Under **the Beneficiary's bank details** there should be an option for the user to enter a Bank SWIFT/BIC code. A valid SWIFT/BIC code should have: • first 4-letter as bank code • then 2-letter for country code • then 2-letter or number location code • followed by 3-letter or number for branch code (optional)	TC_09	Verify IMT Main Screen_6	To verify the user can only enter a valid SWIFT/BIC code in bank SWIFT/BIC code field
R2.7	Under the **Beneficiary's details,** there should be an option for the user to enter the beneficiary's name which can be a maximum of 25 characters.	TC_10	Verify IMT Main Screen_7	To verify the user can enter a beneficiary name and validation for the field
R2.8	Under the Beneficiary's details, there should be a list of all countries for the user address, the countries which are part of the Sanctions Risk list (SRL) should not show up in the list. IMT system should access the Sanctions Risk list (SRL) from the RISK system in real-time.	TC_11	Verify IMT Main Screen_8	To verify the beneficiary country shows the list of unsanctioned countries

#	Requirement Description	Test case #	Test case Name	High-level test cases
R2.9	Users should be able to select a country for the beneficiary address from the country's dropdown.	TC_12	Verify IMT Main Screen_9	To verify the user can select a country from the beneficiary country list
R2.10	Under **the Beneficiary's details,** there should be an option for the user to enter primary address information which can be a maximum of 25 alphanumeric characters.	TC_13	Verify IMT Main Screen_10	To verify the user can enter a primary address and validation for the field
R2.11	Under **the Beneficiary's details,** there should be an option for the user to enter secondary address information which can be a maximum of 25 alphanumeric characters.	TC_14	Verify IMT Main Screen_11	To verify the user can enter a secondary address and validation for the field
R2.12	Under **the Beneficiary's details,** there should be an option for the user to enter a message for the beneficiary which can be a maximum of 40 alphanumeric characters.	TC_15	Verify IMT Main Screen_12	To verify the user can enter a message for the beneficiary and validation for the field
R2.13	Under **Beneficiary's details** should have an option for the user to enter a description of transfer which can be a maximum of 20 alphanumeric characters.	TC_16	Verify IMT Main Screen__13	To verify the user can enter a description for the transfer and validation for the field
R2.14	After the user has input the mandatory fields on the page, they should have an option to proceed to the next screen.	TC_17	Verify IMT Main Screen_14	To verify the user can proceed to the Transfer detail page
R3.1	If the user entered account number and IBAN are invalid in the Transfer main screen and the user tries to proceed to the next screen • Highlight the field with an exclamation sign • Display error message in red "Account number or IBAN is invalid. Please try again. " • User stays on the **"New international transfer"** screen	TC_18	Verify IMT Main Screen Error Hand_1	To verify the user is shown appropriate error message if the account number and IBAN are invalid and the user can't proceed to the next screen

#	Requirement Description	Test case #	Test case Name	High-level test cases
R3.2	If the user entered SWIFT code is invalid in the Transfer main screen and the user tries to proceed to the next screen • Highlight the field with an exclamation sign • The display error message in red "SWIFT code is invalid. Please try again. " • User stays on the "**New international transfer**" main screen	TC_19	Verify IMT Main Screen Error Hand_2	To verify the user is shown appropriate error message if the SWIFT code is invalid and the user can't proceed to the next screen
R4.1	Under **Transfer details,** there should be an option for the user to enter the amount which can be greater than or equal to 10 and less than and equal to the daily IMT limit set by the bank (check the daily IMT limit in RISK system the current limit is AUD 10,000)	TC_20	Verify Transfer Detail screen_1	To verify the user can enter the amount for transfer which is within the limits
R4.2	Under **Transfer details,** the standard international fee should be auto-populated after the user enter the amount (check the RISK system for standard fees). This should be a non-editable field.	TC_21	Verify Transfer Detail screen_2	To verify standard international fee is populated
R4.3	Under **Transfer details,** the user should be displayed the total cost after they enter the amount. This should be auto-populated with the sum of the amount and the standard international fee. This should be a non-editable field.	TC_22	Verify Transfer Detail screen_3	To verify the total amount is populated
R4.4	The current exchange rate for the beneficiary currency from SWIFT should be displayed as the current rate for the user. This should be a non-editable field.	TC_23	Verify Transfer Detail screen_4	To verify the current exchange rate is populated from SWIFT
R4.5	The current date time when the exchange rate is retrieved from SWIFT should be displayed for the user. This should be a non-editable field.	TC_24	Verify Transfer Detail screen_5	To verify current datetime is populated from SWIFT

#	Requirement Description	Test case #	Test case Name	High-level test cases
R4.6	The user should be displayed the auto-populated what beneficiary will receive which should be the total cost * current rate. This should be a non-editable field.	TC_25	Verify Transfer Detail screen_6	To verify what beneficiary will receive field is populated
R4.7	Under **Transfer details,** the user should be provided an option to select whether the fees should be deducted from the total amount or as an extra from the sending account	TC_26	Verify Transfer Detail screen_7	To verify the user can select whether the fees should be deducted from the total amount or as an extra from the sending account
R4.8	Under **Transfer details,** the user should be provided an option to view the terms and conditions for international money transfer	TC_27	Verify Transfer Detail screen_8	To verify the link for terms and conditions page
R4.9	International transfer terms and conditions should be the same as the terms and conditions defined in the RISK system.	TC_28	Verify Transfer Detail screen_9	To verify terms and conditions page content
R4.10	There should be an option for the user to acknowledge that they have read and agreed to the terms and conditions	TC_29	Verify Transfer Detail screen_10	To verify the user can accept terms and conditions
R4.11	There should be an option for the user to go back and change the details on the previous screen. All previous pages should default to the values entered previously.	TC_30	Verify Transfer Detail screen_11	To verify the user can go back to the new International detail page
R4.12	After the user has input the valid amount and acknowledged the terms and conditions, they should have an option to proceed to the next screen	TC_31	Verify Transfer Detail screen_12	To verify the user can proceed to the Transfer confirmation page
R5.1	If the user entered amount is less than 10 (minimum limit in RISK system) and the user tries to proceed to the next screen • Highlight the field with an exclamation sign • Display error message "Amount less than the minimum limit. Please try again. "in red text • User stays on the **"New international transfer detail"** screen	TC_32	Verify Transfer Detail Screen Error Hand_1	To verify bank minimum limit is enforced for user input amount field

#	Requirement Description	Test case #	Test case Name	High-level test cases
R5.2	If the Total amount is greater than the account balance and the user tries to proceed to the next screen • Highlight the field with an exclamation sign • Display error message "Amount greater than the Account balance. Please try again. "in red text • User stays on the **"New international transfer detail"** screen	TC_33	Verify Transfer Detail Screen Error Hand_2	To verify that the user can proceed if the total amount is greater than the account balance
R5.3	If the user entered amount is greater than the IMT limit in RISK system (current limit AUD 10,000) and the user tries to proceed to the next screen • Highlight the field with an exclamation sign • Display error message "Amount greater than the maximum limit. Please try again. "in red text • User stays on the **"New international transfer detail"** screen	TC_34	Verify Transfer Detail Screen Error Hand_3	To verify bank maximum limit is enforced for user input amount field
R5.4	If the user has not entered the amount and the user tries to proceed to the next screen • Highlight the field with an exclamation sign • Display error message "Please enter the amount and try again. "in red text • User stays on the **"New international transfer detail"** screen	TC_35	Verify Transfer Detail Screen Error Hand_4	To verify the user cannot proceed to transfer confirmation page unless they have completed all mandatory fields in Transfer detail page
R5.5	When the user tries to proceed to the next screen and the user has not acknowledged the terms and conditions • Highlight the field with an exclamation sign • Display error message "Please acknowledge terms and conditions. "in red text • User stays on the **"New international transfer detail"** screen	TC_36	Verify Transfer Detail Screen Error Hand_5	To verify the user can proceed to transfer confirmation page once they have completed all mandatory fields in Transfer detail page

#	Requirement Description	Test case #	Test case Name	High-level test cases
R6.1	Under **view and confirm your transfer** the user should be able to view the amount which should be same as the Total amount from in the **transfer detail screen** which is non-editable	TC_37	Verify Transfer Confirmation Screen_1	To verify Amount in the Transfer Confirmation Page
R6.2	Under **view and confirm your transfer** the user should be able to view the **from account** selected in the **transfer main screen** for payment which is non-editable	TC_38	Verify Transfer Confirmation Screen_2	To verify From Account in the Transfer Confirmation Page
R6.3	Under **view and confirm your transfer** the user should be able to view the **beneficiary account** entered in the **transfer detail screen** which is non-editable	TC_39	Verify Transfer Confirmation Screen_3	To verify To Account in the Transfer Confirmation Page
R6.4	Under view and confirm your transfer the user should be displayed the payment date which should be the Today Date + 2-3 business Days non-editable (Weekend and public holidays are considered as non-business days)	TC_40	Verify Transfer Confirmation Screen_4	To verify Payment date in the Transfer Confirmation Page
R6.5	Following disclaimer should be displayed to the user after the payment date: "It takes 2-3 business days to process international transfers Important: Please check that the account details are correct. We may not be able to recover funds sent to the wrong account."	TC_41	Verify Transfer Confirmation Screen_5	To verify disclaimer in the Transfer Confirmation Page
R6.6	There should be an option for the user to go back and change the details on the previous screen. All previous pages should default to the values entered previously.	TC_42	Verify Transfer Confirmation Screen_6	To verify back button functionality in the Transfer Confirmation Page
R6.7	The user should be provided with an option to confirm the payment and proceed to the next screen.	TC_43	Verify Transfer Confirmation Screen_7	To verify confirm button functionality in the Transfer Confirmation Page

#	Requirement Description	Test case #	Test case Name	High-level test cases
R7.1	On the **Receipt page,** the user should be displayed in the following fields based on the selection and entry from the previous screens • Amount • Updated balance • From • To • Payment date All the above fields should be non-editable.	TC_44	Verify Transfer Receipt screen_1	To verify the values on Transfer Receipt Page
R7.2	The user should be provided a receipt number which is a unique 12-digit alphanumeric value auto-generated by the system	TC_45	Verify Transfer Receipt screen_2	To verify the receipt number on Transfer Receipt Page
R7.3	The user should be provided an option to print the confirmation details.	TC_46	Verify Transfer Receipt screen_3	To verify the print functionality on Transfer Receipt Page
R7.4	The confirmation details should be provided to the user as a new mail in the internet banking mailbox.	TC_47	Verify Transfer Receipt screen_4	To verify the user receives the new confirmation mail after International fund transfer

20 Low-Level Test Cases

After the high-level test cases are reviewed testers can start working on the low-level test cases or test scripts which provides step by step details for the test execution. Once the low-level test cases are ready, they are included as a part of a test suite. The test suite is the collection of test cases with the priorities of test cases and order of sequence. Generally, in large projects, where multiple testers are involved, it is common that the testers may execute the test cases written by other testers. Therefore, the test cases should have all the detailed information to successfully execute the test cases without referring to the test basis (business requirement or design documents). This detailed information is also helpful later when these test cases are included as part of the regression testing for future releases or automated by the automation team.

Below are some of the low-level test cases (test scripts) for IMT functionality, different organizations may have different templates, in most projects, a testing tool is used to store the test cases to allow easy traceability to the requirements and automatic version control.

Following abbreviations are used in the Test Case template:

P -Priority of test case

1: **High-risk areas for business**- All test cases under this category **Must** be executed

2: **Medium risk areas for business** – All test cases under this category should be executed if time permits.

3: **Low-risk areas for business**- All test cases under this category if not executed will not have any major impact on the release

PREQ- Prerequisite or precondition for executing the test case

REQS- Requirements (Mapping to the requirement from BRD)

TC- Test case

TC ID	TC Name	Objective	REQS	Step No.	Test Step Description	Expected Results	P
TC_01	Verify IMT Menu_1	To verify user entitled for International transfer can see the 'New International Transfer' menu item	R1.1	PREQ	User entitled for International transfer has logged in to GS Online Banking page	User is on the Account landing page	1
				Step1	User click on 'Fund transfer' menu item	User can see a "**New International Transfer**" menu after "New multiple funds transfer"	
TC_02	Verify IMT Menu_2	To verify user not entitled for International transfer cannot see the 'New International Transfer' menu item	R1.1	PREQ	User not entitled for International transfer has logged in to GS Online Banking page	User is on the Account landing page	1
				Step1	User click on 'Fund transfer' menu item	User is not able to see the "**New International Transfer**" menu	
TC_03	Verify IMT Menu_3	To verify the user is navigated to 'New International Transfer' main screen	R1.2	PREQ	User entitled for International transfer has logged in to GS Online Banking page	User is on the Account landing page	1
				Step1	User click on 'Fund transfer' menu item	User can see a "**New International Transfer**" menu after "New multiple funds transfer"	
				Step2	User click on "**New International Transfer**" menu	User should be navigated to New International Transfer page	
TC_04	Verify IMT Main Screen_1	To verify user account details are populated on 'New International Transfer' main screen	R2.1	PREQ	User has clicked on the "**New International Transfer**" menu and is on New International Transfer page		1
				Step1	Verify the customer name	It is auto-populated and same as the customer name from the online banking account page	

TC ID	TC Name	Objective	REQS	Step No.	Test Step Description	Expected Results	P
TC_05	Verify IMT Main Screen_2	To verify the user can select the eligible account as a from account for the International transfer	R2.2	PREQ	User having a checking, saving, credit card, and a mortgage account has clicked on "**New International Transfer**" menu and is on New International Transfer page		1
				Step1	Check the **"From account"** dropdown & select an account	Only checking accounts should be there in the dropdown. The saving, mortgage account, and credit card should not be there in the drop¬down. The user is able to select an account from the dropdown.	1
TC_06	Verify IMT Main Screen_3	To verify only the eligible country for transfers are displayed in the beneficiary bank location dropdown	R2.3	PREQ	User has clicked on the "**New International Transfer**" menu and is on New International Transfer page		1
				Step1	Check the "**Beneficiary's bank location**" dropdown	The dropdown should have the same list of countries eligible for international transfer from the RISK system.	1
TC_07	Verify IMT Main Screen_4	To verify the user can select a country from the beneficiary bank location dropdown	R2.4	PREQ	User has clicked on the "**New International Transfer**" menu and is on New International Transfer page		1
				Step1	Select the location from the "**Beneficiary's bank location**" dropdown	The user can select the location from the dropdown.	1

TC ID	TC Name	Objective	REQS	Step No.	Test Step Description	Expected Results	P
TC_08	Verify IMT Main Screen_5	To verify the user can only enter a valid account number or IBAN in beneficiary bank details	R2.5	PREQ	User has clicked on the "**New International Transfer**" menu and is on New International Transfer page		1
				Step1	Try to enter the alphabets in the account number or IBAN field.	The field should not accept alphabets	
				Step2	Try to enter an account number more than 12 digits	The field should not accept any digit after the 12th digit.	
				Step3	Try to enter a valid account number which is up to 12 digits	The field should accept the account number.	
TC_09	Verify IMT Main Screen_6	To verify the user can only Enter a valid SWIFT/BIC code e.g. USBKU-S44IMT in bank SWIFT/BIC code field	R2.6	PREQ	User has clicked on the "**New International Transfer**" menu and is on New International Transfer page		1
				Step1	Try entering special characters in the SWIFT/BIC code field	The field should not accept special characters.	
				Step2	Enter a SWIFT/BIC code with more than 12 digits	The field should not accept any digit after the 12th digit.	
				Step3	Enter a valid SWIFT/BIC code	The field should accept the code.	

TC ID	TC Name	Objective	REQS	Step No.	Test Step Description	Expected Results	P
TC_10	Verify IMT Main Screen_7	To verify the user can enter a beneficiary name and validation for the field	R2.7	PREQ	User has clicked on the "**New International Transfer**" menu and is on New International Transfer page		1
				Step1	Try to enter a Beneficiary's name with more than 25 characters	The field should not accept any new character after the 25th character.	
				Step2	Try to enter a special character in the Beneficiary's name field. E.g. $	User should not be able to enter any special characters in the name field	
				Step3	Try to enter a digit in the Beneficiary's name field. E.g. 9	User should not be able to enter any digit in the name field	
				Step4	Try to enter a Beneficiary's name with spaces in the field	The field should accept the name	
TC_11	Verify IMT Main Screen_8	To verify the beneficiary country shows the list of unsanctioned countries	R2.8	PREQ	User has clicked on the "**New International Transfer**" menu and is on New International Transfer page		1
				Step1	Check the "**country**" dropdown	The dropdown should have the same list of countries eligible for international transfer from the RISK system.	
TC_12	Verify IMT Main Screen_9	To verify the user can select a country from the beneficiary country list	R2.9	PREQ	User has clicked on the "**New International Transfer**" menu and is on New International Transfer page		1
				Step1	Check a country from the "**country**" dropdown	The country should be selected from the dropdown.	

TC ID	TC Name	Objective	REQS	Step No.	Test Step Description	Expected Results	P
TC_13	Verify IMT Main screen_10	To verify the user can enter a primary address and validation for the field	R2.10	PREQ	User has clicked on the "**New International Transfer**" menu and is on New International Transfer page		1
				Step1	Try to enter a primary address with more than 25 characters	The field should not accept any new character after the 25th character.	
				Step2	Try to enter a special character in the Beneficiary's name field. E.g. $	The field should accept the special characters	
				Step3	Try to enter a digit in the Beneficiary's name field. E.g. 9	The field should accept the digits	
				Step4	Try to enter a primary address with spaces	The field should accept the address	
TC_14	Verify IMT Main screen_11	To verify the user can enter a secondary address and validation for the field	R2.11	PREQ	User has clicked on the "**New International Transfer**" menu and is on New International Transfer page		2
				Step1	Try to enter a secondary address with more than 25 characters	The field should not accept any new character after the 25th character.	
				Step2	Try to enter a special character in the Beneficiary's name field. E.g. $	The field should accept the special characters	
				Step3	Try to enter a digit in the Beneficiary's name field. E.g. 9	The field should accept the digits	
				Step4	Try to enter a primary address with spaces	The field should accept the address	

TC ID	TC Name	Objective	REQS	Step No.	Test Step Description	Expected Results	P
TC_15	Verify IMT Main screen_12	To verify the user can enter a message for the beneficiary and validation for the field	R2.12	PREQ	User has clicked on the "**New International Transfer**" menu and is on New International Transfer page		3
				Step1	Try to enter a Message to the beneficiary with more than 40 characters	The field should not accept any new character after the 40th character.	
				Step2	Try to enter a special character in the Message to the beneficiary field. E.g. $	The field should accept the special characters	
				Step3	Try to enter a digit in the message to the beneficiary field. E.g. 9	The field should accept the digits	
				Step4	Try to enter a message to the beneficiary with spaces	The field should accept the message	
TC_16	Verify IMT Main screen_13	To verify the user can enter a description of transfer and validation for the field	R2.13	PREQ	User has clicked on the "**New International Transfer**" menu and is on New International Transfer page		3
				Step1	Try to enter a description of transfer with more than 20 characters	The field should not accept any new character after the 20th character.	
				Step2	Try to enter a special character in the description of the transfer field. E.g. $	The field should accept the special characters	
				Step3	Try to enter a digit in the Description of the transfer field. E.g. 9	The field should accept the digits	
				Step4	Try to enter a message in the description of transfer with spaces	The field should accept the message	

TC ID	TC Name	Objective	REQS	Step No.	Test Step Description	Expected Results	P
TC_17	Verify IMT main screen_14	To verify the user can proceed to the Transfer detail page	R2.14	PREQ	User has clicked on the "**New International Transfer**" menu and is on New International Transfer page		1
				Step1	User has entered all the mandatory fields in the page and clicked on the Next button	The user is landed on the Transfer details page.	
TC_18	Verify IMT Main Screen Error Hand_1	To verify the user is shown appropriate error message if the account number and IBAN are invalid and the user can't proceed to the next screen	R3.1	PREQ	User has clicked on the "**New International Transfer**" menu and is on New International Transfer page		1
				Step1	User complete all the mandatory fields in the Transfer main screen and enter invalid account number e.g. 000000 or 1234 (less than six digits)	• The Account number or IBAN field is highlighted in red with exclamation sign in the end. • Error message "Account number or IBAN is invalid. Please try again. "is displayed below the field. • User stays on the "**New international transfer**" screen	
				Step2	User complete all the mandatory fields in the Transfer main screen and enter invalid IBAN code e.g. xxx232343 and click on next button	• The Account number or IBAN field is highlighted in red with exclamation sign in the end. • Error message "Account number or IBAN is invalid. Please try again. "is displayed below the field. • User stays on the "**New international transfer**" screen	

TC ID	TC Name	Objective	REQS	Step No.	Test Step Description	Expected Results	P
TC_19	Verify IMT Main Screen Error Hand_2	To verify the user is shown appropriate error message if the SWIFT code is invalid and the user can't proceed to the next screen	R3.2	PREQ	User has clicked on the "**New International Transfer**" menu and is on New International Transfer page		1
				Step1	The user completes all the mandatory fields in the Transfer main screen and enters invalid SWIFT code. E.g. TEST123	• The SWIFT code field is highlighted in red with an exclamation sign in the end. • Error message "SWIFT code is invalid. Please try again." is displayed below the field. • User stays on the "New international transfer" screen	
TC_20	Verify Transfer Detail screen_1	To verify the user can enter the amount for transfer which is within the limits	R4.1	PREQ	The user has completed all the details on the New International Transfer page and is on the Transfer details screen.		1
				Step1	Try to enter a special character in the Amount field. E.g. -, $	The field should not allow entering special characters in the amount field	
				Step2	Try to enter an alphabet in the **Amount** field. E.g. a, z	The field should not allow entering alphabet in the amount field	
				Step3	Try to enter a digit in the **Amount** field. E.g. 100	The field should accept the digits	
TC_21	Verify Transfer Detail screen_2	To verify standard international fee is populated	R4.2	PREQ	The user has completed all the details on the New International Transfer page and is on the Transfer details screen.		1
				Step1	User has entered a valid amount in the Amount field	The standard international fee is auto-populated. The field is non-editable, and the value of the field should be the same as the standard international transfer fee from the RISK system.	

TC ID	TC Name	Objective	REQS	Step No.	Test Step Description	Expected Results	P
TC_22	Verify Transfer Detail screen_3	To verify the total amount is populated	R4.3	PREQ	The user has completed all the details on the New International Transfer page and is on the Transfer details screen.		1
				Step1	Check the total cost field.	• The value should be auto-populated after the user has entered the amount. • The value of this field is the sum of the amount and the standard international fee. (when the radio button for the "Fees will be deducted from" is selected as "The account above") • The value of this field is equal to the amount. (If the user has selected the fees will be deducted from- The funds, I'm sending radio button) • The user is not able to edit this field.	
TC_23	Verify Transfer Detail Screen_4	To verify the current exchange rate is populated from SWIFT	R4.4	PREQ	The user has completed all the details on the New International Transfer page and is on the Transfer details screen.		1
				Step1	Check the current exchange field.	• The value should be auto-populated. • The value of this field should be the same as the current rate from the SWIFT system. • User is not able to edit this field	

TC ID	TC Name	Objective	REQS	Step No.	Test Step Description	Expected Results	P
TC_24	Verify Transfer Detail Screen_5	To verify current date-time is populated from SWIFT	R4.5	PREQ	The user has completed all the details on the New International Transfer page and is on the Transfer details screen.		1
				Step1	Check the current date-time field.	• The value should be auto-populated. • The value of this field should show the date & time when the exchange rate is retrieved from the SWIFT system. • The date-time should not be **less than 30 mins** from the current online banking server date time. • User is not able to edit this field	
TC_25	Verify Transfer Detail Screen_6	To verify what beneficiary will receive field is populated	R4.6	PREQ	The user has completed all the details on the New International Transfer page and is on the Transfer details screen.		2
				Step1	Check the Beneficiary Received field.	• The value should be auto-populated. • The value of this field should be equal to the (Amount x Current rate). • User is not able to edit this field	

TC ID	TC Name	Objective	REQS	Step No.	Test Step Description	Expected Results	P
TC_26	Verify Transfer Detail Screen_7	To verify the user can select whether the fees should be deducted from the total amount or as an extra from the sending account	R4.7	PREQ	The user has completed all the details on the New International Transfer page and is on the Transfer details screen.		2
				Step1	Check the default radio button for the 'Fees will be deducted from' field	The default value should be "The funds I'm sending"	
				Step2	User tries to change the selection for the radio button for the 'Fees will be deducted from' field to "The funds I'm sending"	User can change the selection	
				Step3	Check the value of the Total cost field after changing the selection	The value of this field should be the sum of the amount and the standard international fee.	
				Step4	Change the radio button to "The funds I'm sending"	The value of this field should be equal to the amount field now.	
TC_27	Verify Transfer Detail Screen_8	To verify the link for terms and conditions page	R4.8	PREQ	The user has completed all the details on the New International Transfer page and is on the Transfer details screen.		1
				Step1	Check if there is a link for terms and conditions	• There should be a link for the terms and conditions in the Terms and conditions section. • Once user click on the link they are directed to terms and condition page	

TC ID	TC Name	Objective	REQS	Step No.	Test Step Description	Expected Results	P
TC_28	Verify Transfer Detail Screen_9	To verify terms and conditions page content	R4.9	PREQ	The user has completed all the details on the New International Transfer page and is on the Transfer details screen. User has clicked on the terms and conditions link		1
				Step1	Check the content of the terms and conditions page	The content of terms and conditions should be the same as International Transfer Terms and conditions in the RISK system.	
TC_29	Verify Transfer Detail screen_10	To verify the user can accept terms and conditions	R4.10	PREQ	The user has completed all the details on the New International Transfer page and is on the Transfer details screen.		1
				Step1	Check the default status of the terms and conditions checkbox	By default, the terms and conditions checkbox should not be checked	
				Step2	Try to select the terms and conditions checkbox	The user can check-in the checkbox and a tick is visible in the box.	
TC_30	Verify Transfer Detail screen_11	To verify the user can go back to the new International detail page	R4.11	PREQ	The user has completed all the details on the New International Transfer page and is on the Transfer details screen.		1
				Step1	Click on the back button	• The user is transferred to the New International detail page. • All the information entered by the user are retained in the page • User can modify any of the information entered before	

TC ID	TC Name	Objective	REQS	Step No.	Test Step Description	Expected Results	P
TC_31	Verify Transfer Detail screen_12	To verify the user can proceed to the Transfer confirmation page	R4.12	PREQ	The user has completed all the details on the New International Transfer page and is on the Transfer details screen.		1
				Step1	User has entered the valid amount and clicked on the terms and conditions checkbox and clicked on the Next button	The user is landed on the Transfer confirmation page.	
TC_32	Verify Transfer Detail Screen Error Hand_1	To verify bank minimum limit is enforced for user input amount field	R5.1	PREQ	The user has completed all the details on the New International Transfer page and is on the Transfer details screen.		1
				Step1	User entered amount as 9.99 (value exactly before the boundary value of 10)	• The Amount field is highlighted in red with an exclamation sign in the end. • Error message "Amount less than the minimum limit. Please try again." is displayed below the field. • User stays on the "**Transfer Detail**" screen	
				Step2	User entered amount as 10.00 (value exactly at the boundary value of 10)	• There is no error message displayed • The user is landed on the Transfer confirmation page.	
				Step3	User entered amount as 10.01 (value above the boundary value of 10)	• There is no error message displayed • The user is landed on the Transfer confirmation page.	

TC ID	TC Name	Objective	REQS	Step No.	Test Step Description	Expected Results	P
TC_33	Verify Transfer Detail Screen Error Hand_2	To verify that the user cannot proceed if the total amount is greater than the account balance	R5.2	PREQ	The user has completed all the details on the New International Transfer page and is on the Transfer details screen.		
				Step1	Total cost is 1 cent less than the amount balance (value exactly before the boundary value) e.g. if the balance is $100 and the total amount calculated based on the input is $99.99.	• There is no error message displayed • The user is landed on the Transfer confirmation page.	
				Step2	User entered amount equal to the account balance (value exactly at the boundary value)	• There is no error message displayed • The user is landed on the Transfer confirmation page.	1
				Step3	Total cost is 1 cent more than the amount balance (value exactly above the boundary value) e.g. if the balance is $100 and the total amount calculated based on the input is $100.01.	• The Amount field is highlighted in red with an exclamation sign in the end. • Error message "Amount greater than the Account balance. Please try again." is displayed below the field. • User stays on the **"Transfer Detail"** screen	

TC ID	TC Name	Objective	REQS	Step No.	Test Step Description	Expected Results	P
TC_34	Verify Transfer Detail Screen Error Hand_3	To verify bank maximum limit is enforced for user input amount field	R5.3	PREQ	The user has completed all the details on the New International Transfer page and is on the Transfer details screen.		1
				Step1	User entered amount as 9999.99 (value exactly before the boundary value of 10,000)	• There is no error message displayed • The user is landed on the Transfer confirmation page.	
				Step2	User entered amount as 10,000 (value exactly at the boundary value of 10,000)	• There is no error message displayed • The user is landed on the Transfer confirmation page.	
				Step3	User entered amount as 10,000.01 (value above the boundary value of 10,000)	• The Amount field is highlighted in red with an exclamation sign in the end. • Error message "Amount greater than the maximum limit. Please try again. "is displayed below the field. • User stays on the "Transfer Detail" screen	

TC ID	TC Name	Objective	REQS	Step No.	Test Step Description	Expected Results	P
TC_35	Verify Transfer Detail Screen Error Hand_4	To verify the user cannot proceed to transfer confirmation page unless they have completed all mandatory fields in Transfer detail page	R5.4	PREQ	The user has completed all the details on the New International Transfer page and is on the Transfer details screen.		1
				Step1	User has not entered the amount and not checked in the terms and conditions checkbox and clicked on the Next button	• I have read terms and conditions and the amount field is highlighted in red with exclamation sign in the end. • Error message "Please agree to the terms and con¬ditions." is displayed below the terms and conditions field in red. • Error message "Please enter the amount and try again." is displayed below the field in red. • User stays on the "**Transfer De-tail**" screen	
				Step2	User has not entered the amount but has checked in the terms and conditions checkbox and clicked on the Next button	• The Amount field is highlighted in red with an exclamation sign in the end. • Error message "Please enter the amount and try again." is displayed below the field. • User stays on the "**Transfer De-tail**" screen	
TC_36	Verify IMT Main Screen Error Hand_5	To verify the user can proceed to transfer confirmation page once they have completed all mandatory fields in Transfer detail page	R5.5	PREQ	The user has completed all the details on the New International Transfer page and is on the Transfer details screen.		1
				Step1	User has entered the amount but not checked in the terms and conditions checkbox and clicked on the Next button	• I have read terms and conditions is highlighted in red with exclamation sign in the end. • Error message "Please agree to the terms and conditions." is displayed below the field in red. • User stays on the "**Transfer De-tail**" screen	

TC ID	TC Name	Objective	REQS	Step No.	Test Step Description	Expected Results	P
TC_37	Verify Transfer Confirm Screen_1	To verify Amount in the Transfer Confirmation Page	R6.1	PREQ	The user has completed all the details on the New International Transfer page and detail page and is on the Transfer Confirmation screen.		
				Step1	Check the amount displayed in the **amount** field	• The account selected should be the same as the Total amount from the Transfer detail page • User should not be able to edit the field values	1
TC_38	Verify Transfer Confirm Screen_2	To verify From Account in the Transfer Confirmation Page	R6.2	PREQ	The user has completed all the details on the New International Transfer page and detail page and is on the Transfer Confirmation screen.		
				Step1	Check the account displayed in the **from account** field	• The account selected should be the same as the account selected in the Transfer main page • User should not be able to edit the field values	1
TC_39	Verify Transfer Confirm Screen_3	To verify To Account in the Transfer Confirmation Page	R6.3	PREQ	The user has completed all the details on the New International Transfer page and detail page and is on the Transfer Confirmation screen.		
				Step1	Check the account displayed in the **beneficiary account** field	• The account selected should be the same as the **beneficiary account** from the Transfer main page • User should not be able to edit the field values	1

TC ID	TC Name	Objective	REQS	Step No.	Test Step Description	Expected Results	P
TC_40	Verify Transfer Confirm Screen_4	To verify Payment date in the Transfer Confirmation Page	R6.4	PREQ	The user has completed all the details on the New International Transfer page and detail page and is on the Transfer Confirmation screen.		2
				Step1	Check the date displayed in the payment date field	• The date should be displayed as the current system date from RISK system + 2-3 business days • User should not be able to edit the field values	
TC_41	Verify Transfer Confirm Screen_5	To verify disclaimer in the Transfer Confirmation Page	R6.5	PREQ	The user has completed all the details on the New International Transfer page and detail page and is on the Transfer Confirmation screen.		1
				Step1	Check the disclaimer after the payment date	The disclaimer should be "It takes 2-3 business days to process international transfers Important: Please check that the account details are correct. We may not be able to recover funds sent to the wrong account."	
TC_42	Verify Transfer Confirm Screen_6	To verify back button functionality in the Transfer Confirmation Page	R6.6	PREQ	The user has completed all the details on the New International Transfer page and detail page and is on the Transfer Confirmation screen.		2
				Step1	Click on the back button	• The user is on the Transfer detail page. • All the information entered by the user are retained in the page • User can modify any of the information entered previously	

TC ID	TC Name	Objective	REQS	Step No.	Test Step Description	Expected Results	P
TC_43	Verify Transfer Confirm Screen_7	To verify confirm button functionality in the Transfer Confirmation Page	R6.7	PREQ	The user has completed all the details on the New International Transfer page and Transfer details screen and is currently on the Confirmation page.		1
				Step1	The user clicked on the Confirm button.	The user is landed on the Transfer receipt page.	
TC_44	Verify Transfer Receipt Screen_1	To verify the values on Transfer Receipt Page	R7.1	PREQ	User has completed all the details on the New International Transfer page and detail page and confirmed the payment on the confirmation page	The user is currently on the Transfer receipt page	2
				Step1	Check the fields on the Receipt page	• Requested on, Amount, updated balance, From, To and the payment date is the same as the previous pages. • User should not be able to edit the field values	
TC_45	Verify Transfer Receipt Screen_2	To verify the receipt number on Transfer Receipt Page	R7.2	PREQ	User has completed all the details on the New International Transfer page and detail page and confirmed the payment on the confirmation page	The user is currently on the Transfer receipt page	2
				Step1	Check the receipt number displayed	• The field is a 12-digit alphanumeric field • User should not be able to edit the field values	

TC ID	TC Name	Objective	REQS	Step No.	Test Step Description	Expected Results	P
TC_46	Verify Transfer Receipt Screen_3	To verify the print functionality on Transfer Receipt Page	R7.3	PREQ	User has completed all the details on the New International Transfer page and detail page and confirmed the payment on the confirmation page	The user is currently on the Transfer receipt page	3
				Step1	Click on the print button	• The print window is displayed to select the printer	
TC_47	Verify Transfer Receipt screen_4	To verify the user receives the new confirmation mail after International fund transfer	R7.4	PREQ	User has completed all the details on the New International Transfer page and detail page and confirmed the payment on the confirmation page	The user is currently on the Transfer receipt page	3
				Step1	Check the new mail is there for the user as a confirmation	• The user received a new mail in the mailbox • The new mail should have all the details as the confirmation page	

After test cases are written a traceability matrix is prepared which shows the relationships between the requirements and the test cases. It can be used to verify that all the requirements are covered by the test cases. Later if there are any changes to the requirements this matrix can be used to identify the test cases which may need to be modified. Below is the example of one of the traceability matrices where the requirements are in the x-axis and the test cases are on the y-axis.

Requirement Identifiers	Reqs Tested	REQ 1.1	REQ1.2	REQ 1.3	REQ 2.1	REQ 2.2	REQ 2.3.1	REQ 2.3.2	REQ 2.3.3	REQ 2.4	REQ 3.1	REQ 3.2	Continue..	REQ 169.2	REQ 170.1
Test Cases	321	3	2	3	1	1	1	1	1	1	2	3		1	1
TC#1	1	x													
TC#2	2		x	x											
TC#3	2	x													
TC#4	1			x											
TC#5	2	x												x	
TC#6	1		x												
TC#7	1			x											
TC#8	2				x			x							
TC#9	2					x			x						
TC#10	2							x	x						
TC#11	1										x				
TC#12	1										x				
TC#13	1											x			
TC#14	1											x			
TC#15	1											x			
continue...															
TC#345	1														x

Note

There will be more test cases to check the following functionalities:

- Checking the display of the different pages, checking the display of different fields and spelling for the static text within these pages.
- Checking the SWIFT message is created in the correct format and delivered successfully to the SWIFT system.
- Checking the behavior of the system when the transfers are done weekends/ public holidays (non-business days)
- Checking if the information from the IMT system is flowing to other systems within the bank for posting, reporting, accounting, and compliance purpose
- Additional scenarios to cover the product risks mentioned in the Test plan
- And many more to check the negative scenarios to make sure the error handling is proper

In many projects, the UI designer creates the wireframes for the screens so the testers can use them as a reference while writing the test cases to verify the look and feel. Many of the above test cases may also be run with a different set of test customer's accounts and on multiple browsers. More details about the test customer account in the Test data section later.

Note

The test cases where IMT is integrating with other systems i.e. RISK, SWIFT will become part of the System Integration Testing (SIT). The tester doing SIT should have access to the RISK and SWIFT test system to verify the data is flowing correctly to the IMT system. There will also be a few SIT tests around adding few countries in the Sanction Risk List (SRL) in the RISK system and checking that they are now not appearing in the beneficiary bank location dropdown and beneficiary address country dropdown.

21 Test Data

We need a test environment with proper **test data** to execute the test cases prepared for the IMT project. Creating this test data manually is time-consuming and sometimes very difficult as there may be a lot of data dependencies. The easy and more reliable way is to copy the data set from the production system and "scrub" or "anonymize" it to remove any personal information such as Tax File Number (TFN), driver's license, passport number, date of birth, etc., while still maintaining the internal integrity of that data. The scrubbed data can then be used in the testing environment for testing without the risk of a security leak or misuse of personal information. This is particularly important where large volumes of realistic data are required.

Following methods can be used for Data Masking:

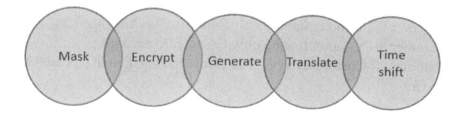

Data Masking

Mask: Masking conceals fields or part of fields with a specific character e.g. * can be used to obscure the actual data e.g. 0426-224-512 can be stored as 0426-***-512.

Encryption: Encryption is the conversion of data into a form, called a ciphertext. This ciphertext is not easily readable and requires a key to decrypt into the original form.

Generate: Generate creates fictitious data or data defined based on a set of rules e.g. comply with a phone number format. Generating can also be conducted on partial fields e.g. for a Passport number field, generating could replace all except the first three characters with fictitious data.

Translate: Replacing sensitive values with meaningful, readable data using a translation table.

Timeshift: Replace sensitive data while maintaining the integrity of a date field (e.g. replace the date of the birth field within a random range of up to ± 6 days from the original date).

Once the test environment is ready with test data, the testers can find the relevant test data which is required for testing. Generally, in large organizations, a separate test data management team manages test data in different environments and can also assist the test team in finding specific test data.

For the IMT project tester would need a variety of customer account to verify that customers can perform IMT transfers only from checking accounts and NOT from savings, mortgage, and credit card accounts.

IMT Testers can find the following type of customers' accounts with suitable balance in the test environment before the start of testing.

1. Customer 1- Customer having Checking account and Mortgage account
2. Customer 2-Customer having Saving account and Mortgage account
3. Customer 3-Customer having Checking, Credit card and Mortgage account
4. Customer 4-Customer having a Credit card and Mortgage account
5. Customer 5-Customer having Checking, Saving, Credit card and Mortgage account
6. Customer 6- Customer having only Mortgage account
7. Customer 7-Customer having only Saving account
8. Customer 8-Customer having only multiple Checking accounts
9. Customer 9-Customer having only Credit card account
10. Customer 10-Customer having Checking, Saving, Credit card and Mortgage account
11. Customer 11-Customer having Checking, Saving, Credit card and Mortgage account – Customer NOT entitled to IMT

Note
It is a good practice to have an extra set of test data before the start of testing. It is very useful when multiple testers are involved in testing and while retesting the defects which may require a different set of test data.

22 | Look and Feel of the System during Test Execution

The following screens show the end-to-end flow of the IMT system with all the relevant error messages with different test accounts.

Global Sun Online banking Login Page

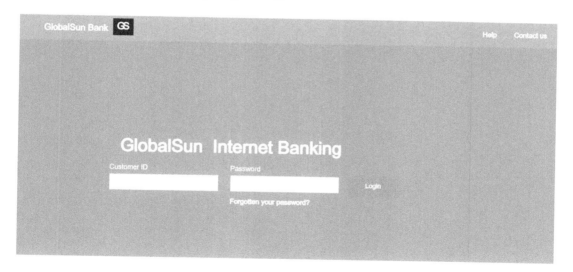

User enter the valid Customer ID and password and click on the Login button

After successful login user is transferred to the Account Summary page

User can see the Account details for their different accounts

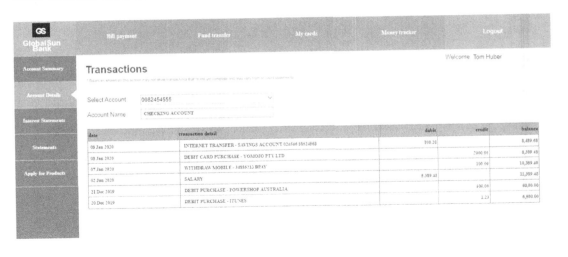

User not entitled for International transfer cannot see the "New International transfer" menu under Fund transfer

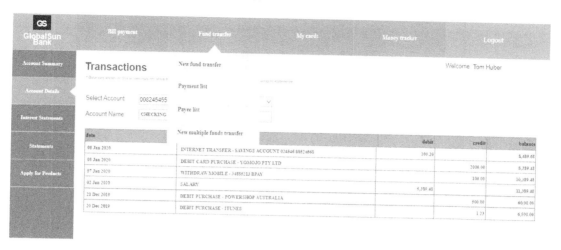

User entitled for International transfer can see the "New International transfer" menu under Fund transfer

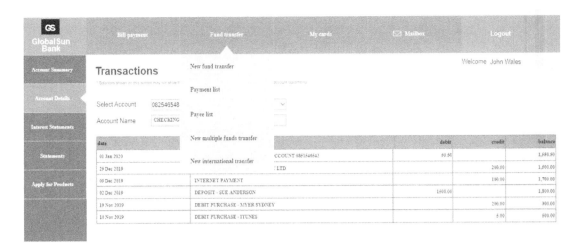

Once the user selects the "New International transfer" menu from Fund Transfer, they are transferred to the New International transfer main page

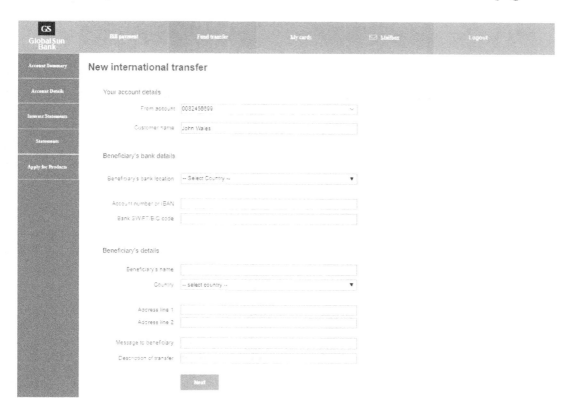

If the user enters wrong Account number or IBAN and clicks on the Next button, the error message is displayed

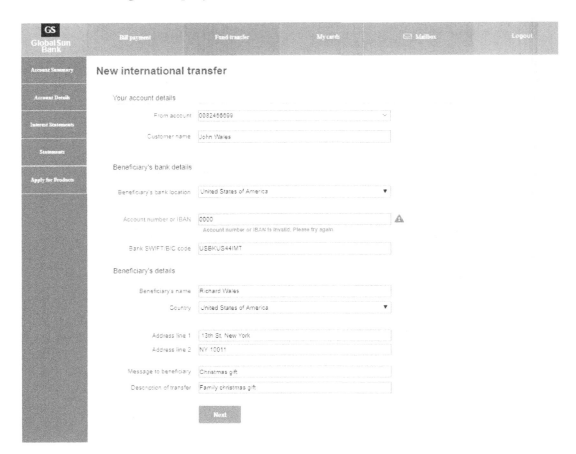

If the user enters an invalid Bank SWIFT/BIC code and clicks on the Next button, the error message is displayed

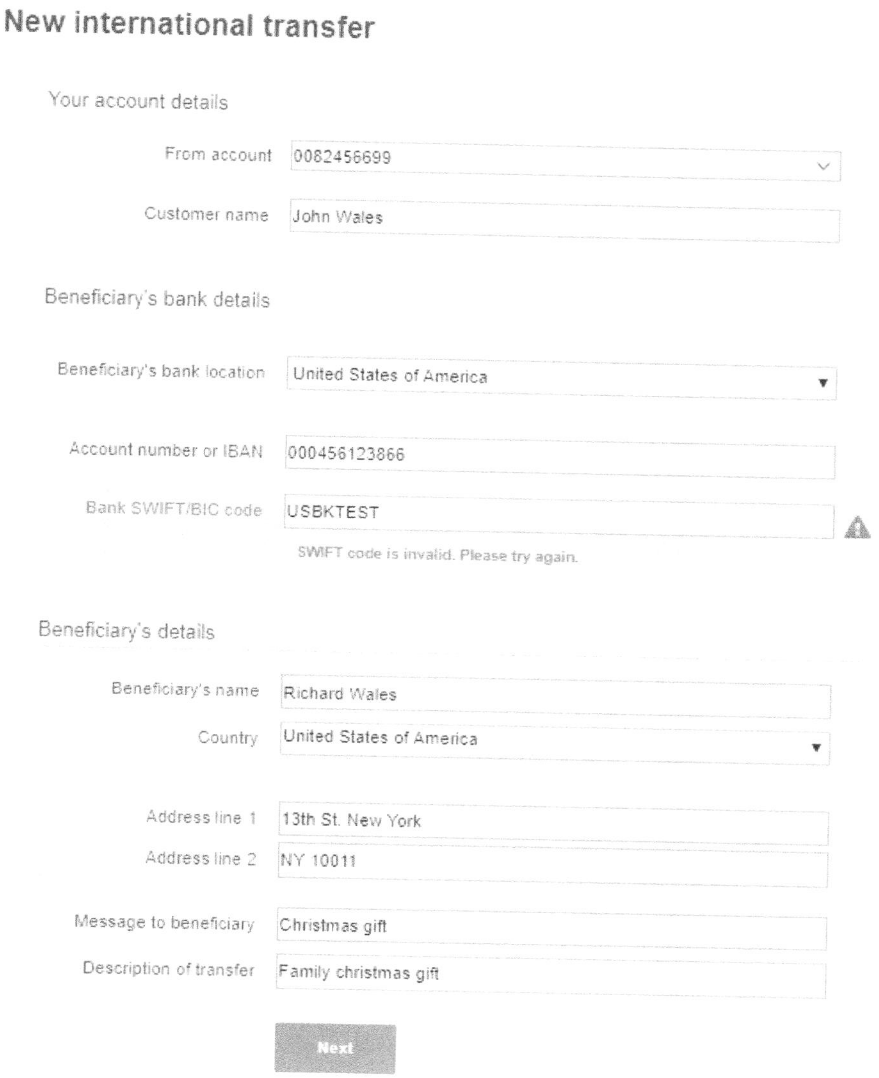

New international transfer

Your account details

From account	0082456699
Customer name	John Wales

Beneficiary's bank details

Beneficiary's bank location	United States of America
Account number or IBAN	000456123866
Bank SWIFT/BIC code	USBKTEST

SWIFT code is invalid. Please try again.

Beneficiary's details

Beneficiary's name	Richard Wales
Country	United States of America
Address line 1	13th St. New York
Address line 2	NY 10011
Message to beneficiary	Christmas gift
Description of transfer	Family christmas gift

Next

After the User fill all mandatory fields on Transfer main page and click on the Next button, they are transferred to the Transfer Detail page

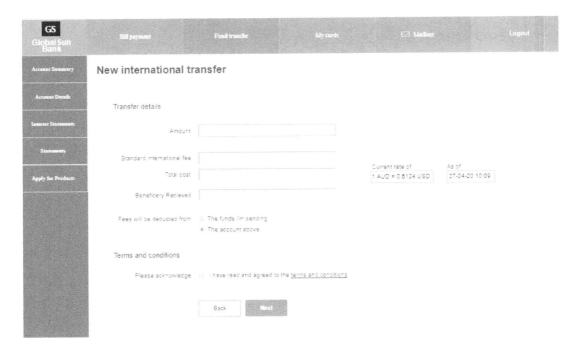

User click on terms and conditions link and a new popup window is displayed

If the User enter Amount more than transfer limit and click on Next button, the error message is displayed

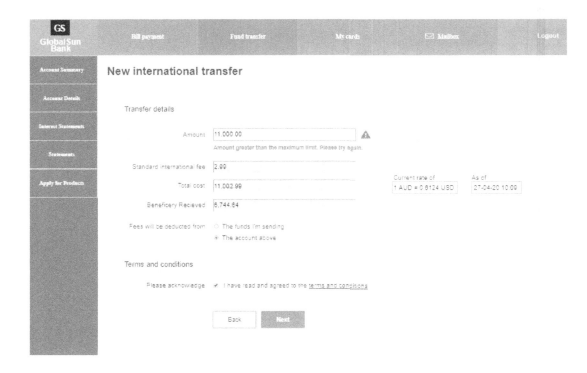

If the user enters amount less than the minimum limit for International transfer and clicks on the Next button, the error message is displayed

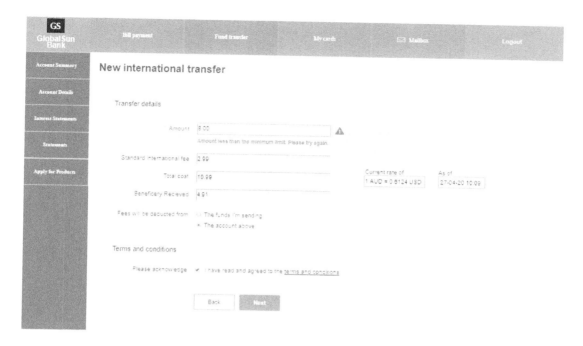

If the User leaves the amount field blank and clicks on the Next button, the error message is displayed

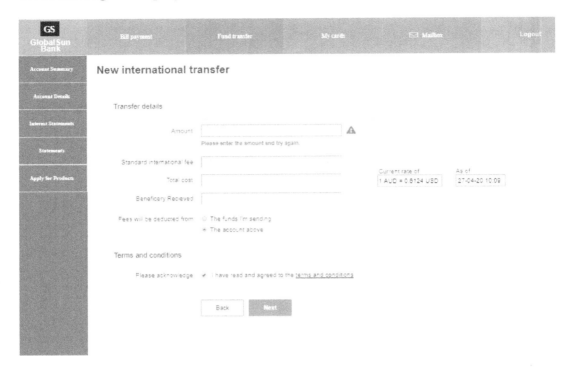

After the user enter all the mandatory fields in Transfer Detail page and click on the Next button, they are transferred to the Transfer confirmation page

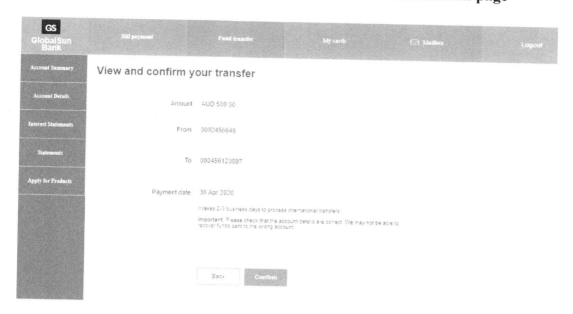

Once the user click on the confirm button, they are transferred to the Transfer Receipt page with a new message in the mailbox

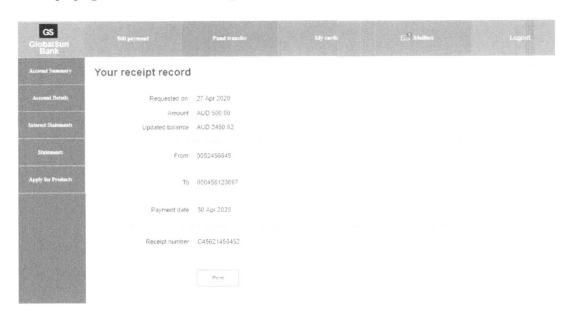

After the User click on the Mailbox menu and select the new mail the receipt for transfer is displayed

Your receipt record

Requested on	27 Apr 2020
Amount	AUD 500.00
Updated balance	AUD 2450.62
From	0082456645
To	000456123897
Payment date	30 Apr 2020
Receipt number	C45621456452

23 Test Execution ST/SIT

Testing can start once all the entry criteria for testing as mentioned in the Test Plan are met i.e. the code build is deployed to the test environment. The testing team generally perform **smoke testing** on the latest build in the testing environment before starting the system testing.

Smoke or Shakedown testing is a quick test to check whether the new software build is actually ready for testing. It is performed whenever the new build is delivered to the test environment. Only after the smoke tests are passed, the full-fledged testing can be started.

The test cases for smoke testing are picked from the System Test suite. The smoke test suite should cover some of the critical tests from end to end flow. A subset of the smoke test can also be used to verify the environment readiness when the new environment is built or updated with a new set of test data.

Now the test cases we have written earlier for IMT functionality can be executed based on dependencies and in the order of priority. Those test cases will be run with multiple customer test accounts and data to verify the functionality. In most of the scenarios, the ST test cases are run first followed by SIT test cases. Occasionally some of the SIT test cases run in parallel to the ST testing as they are part of the end to end flow, the same is applicable for our IMT testing. Only the SIT test cases for downstream i.e. posting etc. can be run after the finish of the ST testing.

ST/SIT testing is an important phase of testing and the successful completion of this phase ensures project success. Test Manager and Test Lead monitor the daily progress of testing to make sure it is progressing as per the initial plan and defects are moving at an acceptable rate. Test execution & defect progress is also shared regularly with the stakeholders using a Test status Report (see Chapter 28).

Note

Smoke testing example

Consider a new web-based system under development. This web-based solution is to capture customer information in three web pages, the first page is for capturing customer personal details, the second page captures customer financial details and the last page is to capture customer assets and liabilities details. After entering all the information, once the customer clicks the submit button on the last page, all this customer information is stored in the database.

System Testing will cover all three pages with different customer types. If the testing team has created 25 test cases of each web page there is a chance that the last page and the submit functionality will be tested very late in the System Testing phase. What if during the last days of testing it is found that the submit functionality is not working? Maybe the submit functionality was not fully developed or properly tested by the development team before the build was delivered.

Now a fix for this critical function may impact a lot of other functionalities for which testing is already completed. Now those test cases have to be **re-executed**. To avoid these types of situations it's better to check the important functions before starting the full fledge system testing. The testing team should have a Smoke Test Suite which verifies these important functions in every new build.

The smoke tests will check all the critical end to end functions with just one customer data. If any of the critical functionality is failing the smoke test status will be considered as FAIL and the build will be rejected. System Testing will not start unless this critical functionality is fixed in the new build.

Defects Found during Test Execution

Below examples shows the different category of defects found during IMT ST/SIT testing:

Critical Severity defect

Defect ID	Defect #11
Defect Type	Functional
Environment	Test Environment
Severity	Critical
Priority	Urgent
Data Raised	03-Apr-xxxx
Summary	User is not able to see IMT link for the customer entitled for IMT transfers
Steps to Reproduce	I. Log in as a user that is entitled to IMT transfers II. In the Account Details page check the International Money Transfer link under Fund transfer tab
Expected Result	International Money Transfer link should be there below New multiple funds transfer
Actual results	International Money Transfer link is not there under Fund transfer
Reference	Requirement- R1.1
Evidence	
Test data	**Customer id**: B501241, **Password**: Passw@rd123

High Severity defect

Defect ID	Defect #37
Defect Type	Functional
Environment	Test Environment
Severity	High
Priority	High
Data Raised	10-Apr-xxxx
Summary	The system is not validating for minimum transfer limit in Transfer Detail page
Steps to Reproduce	I. Log in as a user that is entitled to IMT transfers II. Go to Fund transfer tab and find International Money Transfer link III. Click on the International Money Transfer IV. Put all the details on the New International Transfer page and click on Next button V. In the Transfer Detail page enter the amount as any value less than 10 (RISK system is having minimum transfer limit as 10) VI. Acknowledge the Terms and conditions and click on Next button NOTE- Checked for zero dollars in the amount field and the error message is displayed after the user clicks on the Next button.
Expected Result	The error message should display, and the user should stay on the Transfer detail page
Actual results	There is no error message displayed and the user is progressed to the confirmation page.
Reference	Requirement # R4.1
Evidence	
Test data	**Customer id**: B501241, **Password**: Passw@rd123

Medium Severity defect

Defect ID	Defect #29
Defect Type	Functional
Environment	Test Environment
Severity	Medium
Priority	Low
Data Raised	14-Apr-xxxx
Summary	Back button from Transfer confirmation page not retaining the earlier Transfer details
Steps to Reproduce	I. Login as a user that is entitled to the IMT transfers II. Go to Fund transfer tab and find International Money Transfer link III. Click on the International Money Transfer IV. Put all the bank and beneficiary details on the New International Transfer page and click on Next button V. Enter the Transfer details and acknowledge the Terms and conditions and click on Next button VI. From the view and confirm page click on the back button
Expected Result	User is transferred to the New international transfer page with all the values which were entered previously
Actual results	User is transferred to the New international transfer page, but all the values are not retained (Amount field is blank, and Terms and conditions acknowledgment is unchecked)
Reference	Requirement # R6.6
Evidence	

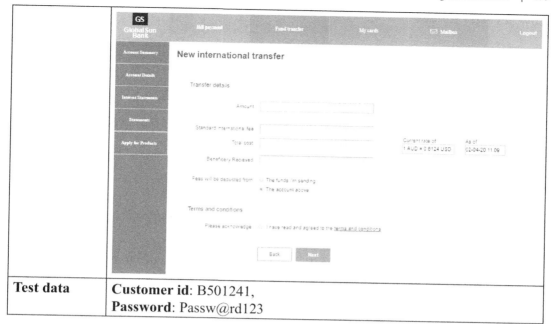

| Test data | **Customer id**: B501241, **Password**: Passw@rd123 |

Low severity defect

Defect ID	Defect #31
Defect Type	Functional
Environment	Test Environment
Severity	Low
Priority	Low
Data Raised	10-Apr-xxxx
Summary	The static label on the Receipt page has a spelling mistake
Steps to Reproduce	I. Log in as a user that is entitled to IMT transfers II. Go to Fund transfer tab and find International Money Transfer link III. Click on the International Money Transfer IV. Put all the details on the New International Transfer page and click on Next button V. Enter the Transfer details and acknowledge the Terms and conditions and click on Next button VI. On the view and confirm page click on Confirm button VII. Check the static labels on the Receipt page
Expected Result	The label for the date should be displayed as "Payment date"
Actual results	The label for the date is displaying as "Pyment date"
Reference	Requirement # R7.1 /General page design functionality
Evidence	
Test data	**Customer id**: B501241, **Password**: Passw@rd123

25 Regression Testing

When the new changes are made to the existing system a type of testing is done to ensure that the changes have not affected any of the current functionality, this testing is called regression testing. The change can be made to the application code due to defect fix or due to the addition of any new functionality. This may also be due to change to the application environment, such as a new version of an operating system or database management system. These changes can have side-effects and may accidentally affect the behavior of other parts of the code, within the same component or in other components of the same system, or even in other systems. Regression testing involves running tests to detect such unintended side-effects.

IMT Regression testing will verify that the IMT code changes have not introduced any new defects in the existing online banking system. Impact Analysis if performed to find which of the existing functionality may be impacted due to the changes, based on this information the test cases are selected from the existing Regression Test suite.

A traceability matrix is prepared to facilitate **Impact analysis**. The traceability matrix can help the testing team to figure out which modules are getting impacted due to the change. Regression test cases should be run for the impacted modules along with other critical end to end regression test scenarios.

The traceability matrix prepared for impact analysis is similar to the one which we have seen in chapter 20. For regression the new changes (new functionality) will be on the x-axis and the regression areas (modules) will be on the y-axis. Generally, the development team will help in preparing the traceability matrix by providing information in the form of **release notes**, these notes will have details of the new changes and which areas and functionalities it may impact.

Note

Regression testing example

Consider a web-based system to capture customer personal information using four screens. It is live-in production and used by the customers. Now the business has requested a new page to be added to the existing system to capture the customer's financial information. The new functionality (Customer Financial Information page) will be part of system testing. The impact analysis will be done to find out which other pages or flow may be affected because of the changes, based on this testing team will pick the relevant regression test cases.

Following are some of the examples of critical test cases for the online banking application which need to be executed as part of regression testing:

TC ID	TC Name	Objective	Step No.	Test Step Description	Expected Results	P
TC_01	Validate Customer Login	To verify the user is able to login to the GS online Banking site using valid credentials	PREQ	User has launched the GS online banking site in the browser and currently on the login page		1
			Step1	The user enters a valid customer ID and password in fields and clicks on the 'Login' button	User is successfully navigated to the Account Summary page	
TC_02	Validate Account Detail Tab	To verify the user is able to see the Account details	PREQ	User has successfully login to GS online banking site and is currently on Account Summary Page		1
			Step1	User click on the Account detail tab on the left and selects an account	The Account name and transactions details related to that account are displayed	
TC_03	Validate Interest Statements	To verify the user is able to see the interest statements for their accounts	PREQ	User has successfully login to GS online banking site and is currently on Account Summary Page

User has a mortgage and saving account | | 1 |
			Step1	User click on the interest statement detail tab on the left and selects saving account from the list	The user is able to see the interest statement for the saving account	
			Step2	The user selects the mortgage account from the list	The user is able to see the interest statement for the mortgage account	
TC_04	Validate Fund Transfer	To verify the user is able to fund transfer to Australian accounts	PREQ	User has successfully login to GS online banking site and is currently on Account Summary Page		1
			Step1	User select New Fund Transfer under Fund Transfer tab and put all the mandatory detail and click on the payment button	Fund transfer is successful, and a receipt page is shown as the final confirmation to the user	
TC_05	Validate Payment List	To verify the user can view the payment list	PREQ	User has successfully login to GS online banking site and is currently on Account Summary Page		1
			Step1	User select Payment list under Fund Transfer tab	The page displays the last 10 payments done by the user.	

And so on...

Note

As the current changes for IMT are related to payments, there will be many more test cases required to check if the current payment functionality for Global Sun online banking is working fine after the IMT changes. Following areas will be a high priority for regression:

- New fund transfer
- Payment list
- Payee list
- New multiple funds transfer
- Bill Payment

26 | UAT Testing

User Acceptance testing or Business verification (BV), typically focuses on the behavior and capabilities of a whole system or product. Objectives of acceptance testing include:

- Establishing confidence in the quality of the system as a whole
- Validating that the system is complete and will work as expected
- Verifying that functional and non-functional behaviors of the system are as specified

Acceptance testing may produce information to assess the system's readiness for deployment and use by the customer (end-user). Defects may be found during acceptance testing, but finding defects is often not an objective, and finding a significant number of defects during acceptance testing may in some cases be considered a major project risk. Acceptance testing may also satisfy legal or regulatory requirements or standards.

Test cases for UAT testing are written based on the customer requirement. These tests should be written and executed by someone who understands the customer requirements and system properly i.e. customer or customer representatives (the business team who works closely with the customer).

The test team may support the UAT testing as the business users are sometimes not aware of the overall UAT test process and testing tools which are used to support this testing. Examples include helping the UAT business testers for environment shakedown tests, creating/finding test data, raising defects in defect tracking tools, assisting them in preparing test status reports, etc.

UAT is performed in the UAT test environment (different from the testing environment) which is more like the real operational production environment with similar test data. These factors help in finding some of the defects which can be replicated only in a production-like environment and/or with production-like data.

The UAT for IMT will focus on end to end positive test scenarios to validate that the new IMT system is complete and working as expected.

27 Non-Functional Testing

For our project IMT so far, we have just discussed the functional testing which is performed to test the overall new functionality. But there are some other types of non-functional testing that are performed before, in parallel to or after the functional testing. These testing are performed by specialist testers. For our IMT project examples of these testing may include:

Usability testing

In a nutshell, this type of testing is done to check how easy it is for the user to use the system with effectiveness, efficiency, and satisfaction.

For the new web pages which are developed as part of IMT, the usability testing will cover the following:

- How easy it is for the user to go through different fields and different pages of the IMT system to do an international transfer.
- Find out any problem that can lead to confusion, error, delay or outright failure to complete the money transfer from the customer point of view.

Performance testing

In a nutshell, this type of testing is done to check the performance of the system when multiple users are logged into the system at normal load and peak load and perform different actions.

For the IMT system, performance testing should cover the following:

- Whether the new system has impacted the performance of the existing Online banking system. This will require comparing the current performance test results with the last performance test results for the online banking system. If the performance is impacted due to the introduction of IMT changes then the root cause should be investigated and fixed before the release.

- As the existing customers will be using the IMT functionality and the bank doesn't see a surge of new customers due to IMT project, load testing is not required for this release.

Security/Penetration testing

In a nutshell, this type of testing is done to identify security vulnerabilities in a system or infrastructure. These tests harden security defences by eliminating vulnerabilities and advising on areas that are susceptible to compromise from attacks from hackers.

For the IMT system, security testing should cover the following:

- To check how vulnerable the new code for IMT is to attack from hackers, as the application is accessible from the internet.
- To check how secure is the data which is transferred between IMT and SWIFT system.
- To gather information about targets and identifying and prioritizing vulnerabilities so proper actions can be taken to fix them before the release.

28 **Test Status Report**

Test Status Report or Test progress report is prepared during a test activity. This is used to communicate to the stakeholder the progress of testing activities and any issues which are hampering the progress of these activities. It contains feedback from the testing team and includes test case execution progress, outstanding defects, risks, and issues. In most of the projects, during the test execution, this report is sent daily to all the relevant stakeholders with the up to date information.

The data in this report is also used to measure exit criteria such as test coverage, e.g. 50 percent requirement coverage achieved. Test Status report should cover ongoing real-time status and results in the easy to understand formats which can be relevant to the project team members and stakeholders. Data should be presented clearly and logically that conveys the appropriate meaning and maps to the initial test objectives and test exit criteria.

The test status report is issued at fixed intervals (daily/weekly) during the test execution as agreed in the Test plan.

Following are common test metrics used in this report:

- Percentage of work done in test case preparation (or percentage of planned test cases prepared)
- Test case execution (e.g. number of test cases run/not run, and test cases passed/failed)
- Defect information (e.g. defect density, defects found and fixed, failure rate and retest results)
- Test coverage of requirements and risks
- Subjective confidence of testers in the system
- Dates of test milestones
- Quality of the test object

Test metrics are used to track progress towards the completion of testing, which is determined by the exit criteria. Therefore, **test metrics should relate directly to the exit criteria.**

Online Banking IMT Release
ST/SIT Test phase
Test Status Report as at Wed 09 APR YYYY

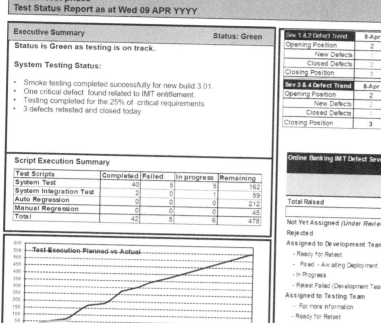

Executive Summary   Status: Green

Status is Green as testing is on track.

System Testing Status:

- Smoke testing completed successfully for new build 3.01.
- One critical defect found related to IMT entitlement.
- Testing completed for the 25% of critical requirements
- 3 defects retested and closed today

Sev 1 & 2 Defect Trend	8-Apr	9-Apr	10-Apr	11-Apr	12-Apr
Opening Position	2	1			
New Defects	1	1			
Closed Defects	2	1			
Closing Position	1	1			

Sev 3 & 4 Defect Trend	8-Apr	9-Apr	10-Apr	11-Apr	12-Apr
Opening Position	2	1			
New Defects	2	2			
Closed Defects	1	2			
Closing Position	3	1			

Script Execution Summary

Test Scripts	Completed	Failed	In progress	Remaining
System Test	40	5	5	162
System Integration Test	2	0	1	59
Auto Regression	0	0	0	212
Manual Regression	0	0	0	45
Total	42	5	6	478

Online Banking IMT Defect Severity grouped by Status

	Sev 1	Sev 2	Sev 3	Sev 4	Total
Total Raised	1	4	7	0	12
Not Yet Assigned *(Under Review)*	0	0	0	0	0
Rejected	0	0	0	0	0
Assigned to Development Team	0	1	2	0	3
- Ready for Retest	0	0	0	0	0
- Fixed - Awaiting Deployment	0	0	0	0	0
- In Progress	0	0	0	0	0
- Retest Failed (Development Team)	0	1	1	0	2
Assigned to Testing Team	0	1	1	0	2
- For more information	0	0	0	0	0
- Ready for Retest	0	2	2	0	4
- In Progress	0	0	0	0	0
- Retest Failed	0	0	0	0	0
Fixed and acceptance tested	0	1	1	0	2
Open Errors	1	1	1	0	3

Test Execution Planned vs Actual (chart, x-axis: 01 Apr, 06 Apr, 11 Apr, 16 Apr, 21 Apr, 26 Apr, 01 May, 06 May, 11 May; y-axis: 0 to 600) — Planned, Actual

Sample daily status report for IMT testing

29 Test Summary Report

Once a testing activity or phase is completed Test Lead or Test Manager issues test summary report for the stakeholders. This report provides a detailed summary of the testing performed, based on the latest test progress report and any other relevant information. It provides a good insight into the testing performed at different levels, information with regards to the defects found during that phase and information regarding outstanding issues and risks which may impact the final release.

One of the important sections in this report is the **"recommendation section"**. In this section based on their confidence in testing and outstanding defects, the testing team provides their recommendations which helps the stakeholders to decide whether it is safe to release this product to production or more work in development and testing is required before that. This information helps the stakeholders to make relevant decisions about the project release.

Below is the Test Summary Report for the IMT projects which covers
ST/SIT/Regression and BV testing phases.

Test Summary Report

Online Banking Release IMT Project

| **Version** | Version 1.0 |
| **Author** | Test Lead |

Table of Contents

Document History

Date	Version	Description	Author
22-May-YYYY	0.1	Initial draft	Test Lead
27-May-YYYY	1.0	Final Version	Test Lead

Document Distribution

Name	Title	Responsibility
	Sponsor of the Program	Sign-Off
	Project Manager	Sign-Off
	Test Manager	Sign-Off
	Development Lead	Review
	Team Leader-Support Services	Review
	Senior Developer- IT Production	Review
	Testing Team members	Review

1 Introduction

1.1 Document Purpose

This document is intended for:

- Summarizing all test outcomes, outstanding issues and risks for Online Banking Release IMT Project.
- Providing a recommendation for proceeding to Implementation for Online Banking Release IMT Project.
- All Project Stakeholders to review the testing outcomes and assess readiness for Implementation of Online Banking Release IMT Project.
- All project Stakeholders to review the agreed Exit Criteria for Online Banking Release IMT Project in relation to the test outcomes.
- Use as the basis of assessment in the formal "Test Closure" review meeting to assess readiness for Implementation

1.2 Reference Documents

The following documents were referenced in the completion of this Test Summary Report:

Document	Details
Test Strategy	Banking Release IMT Project – Test Strategy v1.0.doc
Test Plan	Banking Release IMT Project – Test Plan v1.0.doc

2 Summary of Testing Effort

2.1 Scope of Testing

The agreed scope for IMT Project as agreed in the Test Strategy is as follows:

Phase	Objective	Scope Inclusions	Scope Exclusions
System Test	Performed by the IMT project Testing team. The objective of this phase is to confirm that the build meets Global Sun functional requirements.	Demonstration of IMT Functionality Execution of system-level test scripts designed to ensure that the new functionality is present and performs operations based on the requirements.	SWIFT interfaces will not be tested
System Integration Test	Performed by IMT project Testing team. • Checks functionality of the integrated system against the business requirements to ensure: • Functions and end to end business processes work as expected • Fields, screens, data integrity and calculations match requirement specifications	End to end testing of all the interfaces mentioned in the Technical Design Document IMT (version 1.0)	none
Regression Test	A set of tests baselined on existing functionality for online banking will be executed to ensure: • Errors have not been introduced • Customer critical functions still work correctly • Commonly used functions still work correctly • High exposure areas still have integrity	All Critical and High Priority Regression scripts will be executed	Medium and Low Priority Regression scripts will only be executed if time permits.
Business Validation	A final validation performed by the Business to ensure a level of comfort prior to implementation. Validation should represent business scenarios performed in end-users day-to-day working life.	End to end business scenarios based on the functional changes implemented with this Release. Validation of high risk and business-critical processes.	Detailed scenario-based functional testing will not be executed during this phase.

2.2 Testing Not Performed

All planned testing in scope was completed.

Note
If any testing is outstanding due to environmental/data issues or any open defects that should be defined in this section.

2.3 Testing Schedule

The agreed test schedule for Online Banking Release IMT Project as represented in Test plan is:

Milestone	Start Date	End Date
ST Test Execution	2nd Apr YYYY	15th Apr YYYY
SIT Test Execution	16th Apr YYYY	27th Apr YYYY
Regression Testing (Manual/ Auto Regression)	28th Apr YYYY	11th May YYYY
BV Testing	13th May YYYY	19th May YYYY

2.4 Testing Environments

ST, SIT, Regression was conducted in the TEST environment and BV testing was conducted in the UAT Environment.

2.5 Testing Resource

Testing was undertaken by resources from:

- ST, SIT, Regression was performed by IMT Testing team
- BV testing was performed by business resources

3   Testing Status

3.1 SIT Test Summary

SIT Test Summary			
	Total No of test scripts executed	Total No of test scripts outstanding	Total No of defects raised
IMT Project ST	160	0	58
IMT Project SIT	62	0	22
Total	222	0	80

3.2 Regression Test Summary

Regression Test Summary			
	Total No of test scripts executed	Total No of test scripts outstanding	Total No of defects raised
Regression-Automation	212	0	3
Regression-Manual	45	0	1
TOTAL	257	0	4

3.3 BV Test Summary

BV Test Summary			
	Total No of test scripts executed	Total No of test scripts outstanding	Total No of defects raised
IMT project-BV	22	0	2
TOTAL	22	0	2

Note
The numbers in the table above are indicative based on the size and complexity of the project.

4   Recommendation

Based on the testing results and the status of outstanding defects, it is recommended that the Global Sun Release IMT Project can be **progressed to the Implementation phase**.

5 Summary of Test Results

5.1 Test Script Summary

Following is a breakdown of test script information per test phase as represented in ALM.

Test Phase	Total Test Scripts	Test Scripts Passed	Test Scripts Failed	Test Scripts could not be run	Test Scripts outstanding
ST	160	160	0	0	0
SIT	62	62	0	0	0
Regression	257	237	0	20	20
BV	22	22	0	0	0

5.2 Summary of Testing Defects

The following section summarizes key defect metrics obtained from ALM for Online Banking Release IMT Project.

5.2.1 Defects by Severity

The following table summarizes defects by Severity across all test phases.

Defect Severity	Test Defects Raised	Test Defects Closed	Test Defects Outstanding
1 = Critical	7	7	0
2 = Major	20	20	0
3 = Minor	49	49	0
4 = Low	10	10	0
TOTAL	86	86	0

5.2.2 Defects by Status

The following table summarizes defects by Status and Severity across all test phases.

Test Phase	Defect Status	Total Defects	A = Critical	B = Major	C = Minor	D = Low
ST/SIT	Closed	80	7	16	42	10
	Deferred	0	0	0	0	0
	Reject	5	0	1	4	0
	Open	0	0	0	0	0
Regression	Closed	4	0	1	3	0
	Deferred	0	0	0	0	0
	Reject	0	0	0	0	0
	Open	0	0	0	0	0
BV	Closed	2	0	2	0	0
	Reject	0	0	0	0	0

5.2.3 Summary of Defects Deferred

The following table summarizes the defects that were deferred as agreed with Stakeholders.

Defect ID	Severity	Summary

Note
There may be some defects that are not impacting the critical functionality and the team is not having much capacity to fix and test them during the current release. In this case, the business can defer these defects to the next release.

5.2.4   List of Defects Rejected

The following table summarizes the defects that were rejected

Defect ID	Severity	Summary

Note
This section will have the list of defects that were rejected during the defect triage meetings. These defects may be raised due to issues with data, environment or wrong test cases or wrong execution of the test cases.

6   Analysis

6.1 Outstanding Issues

The following table summarizes issues outstanding issues as at the completion of testing, with the respective resolutions.

From Test Phase	Issue No	Description / Resolution	Resp.	Impact	Status
Nil					

Note
If there are any defects found during testing which are still open or outstanding, they need to be highlighted in this section.

6.2 Outstanding Risks

The following table summarizes risks outstanding risks as at the completion of testing, with the respective mitigation approach.

From Test Phase	Risk No	Description / Mitigation	Resp.	Impact	Status
Nil					

Note
If any of the risks identified during the start of the project and the ones which are found later and included as a part of the Test Strategy and Test Plan document are not fully covered by testing, they need to be highlighted in this section.

-----------------------End of Test Summary Report-----------------------

30 Release Planning/ Implementation Plan

Though the testing team is not directly responsible to prepare and execute the implementation plan (Runsheet) for the release but there are some activities in which they participate, therefore this knowledge will be helpful when working on a real project.

Release plan/Implementation plan is prepared by the Release team which is agreed and signed off by the business team and all stakeholders.

Following are included as a part of the implementation plan:

- Pre-Release tasks
- Release tasks
- Go/ No-Go decision meeting
- Post-Release tasks which include the Post Verification Testing (PVT) done by business and testing team
- Rollback plan which includes the testing by the project team to make sure all the systems as at pre-release status.

In some of the projects, the new changes are deployed for only some of the selected pilot users which can be internal or low-risk users and then based on their satisfaction after a few days the changes can be deployed for all the users in one go or in a phased manner.

The testing team is responsible for the post verification testing along with business once the new code is deployed into the production environment.

The test case for the PVT testing are prepared during the implementation planning and should be agreed and signed-off by the business.

A sample high-level release plan for IMT project release will be like:

Pre-Release

No	Steps	Responsible	Status
1.	Run E2E Test cases in the TEST environment	Testing team	
2.	Run E2E Test cases in the UAT environment	Business Team	
3.	End to End demo to business in UAT environment	Business Team	
4.	Communicate to all support and development team in the organization about the release plan (so there is no conflict in the production environment during the final deployment)	Release team	

Release

No	Steps	Responsible	Status
1.	Merge code changes	Development Team	
2.	Stop production server	Production support Team	
3.	Backup production database	Production support Team	
4.	Update relevant config in production	Production support Team	
5.	Deploy the newly merged code to production	Production support Team	
6.	Start production server	Production support Team	

Post-Release

No	Steps	Responsible	Status
1.	PVT test for IMT functionality	Testing Team/ Business Team	
2	Quick Regression for online banking functionality	Testing Team/ Business Team	

Go/No-Go Decision

Based on the result of PVT testing it will be decided whether the project can go ahead with the **Planned Release** otherwise the rollback plan needs to be invoked.

Rollback Plan

No.	Activity	Responsible	Status
1.	Restore database.	Production support Team	
2.	Re-deploy previous codebase to the production environment	Production support Team	
3.	Quick Regression for the previous codebase	Testing Team/ Business Team	

Note
These tasks may differ based on the organization and the complexity and size of the project. In some of the organization, PVT is the responsibility of business testers whereas in some organization it is the responsibility of both the business and testing team.

31 Test Closure Activities

After the IMT release code is migrated to the production environment i.e. IMT release is completed, the testing team can start on test completion or closure activities. It involves collecting data from completed test activities to consolidate experience, test-ware, facts, and numbers.

The main Test closure activities testing team will be performing:

1. **Test completion check** – checking that all planned tests are either run or not executed due to any known issues. Verifying that all known defects are either in a fixed or closed state or deferred for a future release.
2. **Test artifacts handover** – Regression test sets (either automated or manual) should be documented and delivered to the BAU team along with other work products.
3. **Lessons learned** – Test Manager/Test Lead will organize a lesson learned meeting with the testing team and other important stakeholders to gather important lessons which can be documented for process improvements. Following items were discussed in the IMT lessons learned meeting:

   - **Checking whether the Testing estimates were accurate?**

     For example, checking whether the estimations done earlier during the start of the project for the testing activities were higher or lower than it should have been? e.g. whether the testing team was able to finish all testing activities on time and any underlying reasons for delays? This will help in future estimation activities.

   - **What are the trends and the results of the cause and effect analysis of the defects?**

     For example, assess if similar defects were found multiple times which can be related to areas of high risk or skills problem.

   - **Are there potential process improvement opportunities?**

     For example, what testing activities should be done in future projects, so similar mistakes are not repeated.

4. **Archiving testing results, project documents, and work products**. If test results and defects are not stored in a Test management tool i.e. ALM they need to be archived along with other work products such as test strategy, test plan, and project plan, with a clear linkage to the system and version they were used on.

32 Recap & Next Steps

I think by now you should have got a fair idea about the sequential software development lifecycle and the corresponding testing activities. The following diagram provides a quick recap of all the phases and activities within each phase.

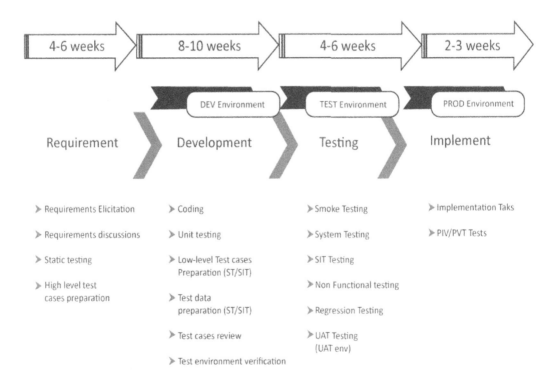

Now looking at the above diagram if you are able to understand each project's tasks, their corresponding testing tasks, the relationship between both, and you are confident that you can comfortably perform, participate and support these testing tasks, you have earned yourself a title of "**Self-Taught Software Tester**".

Now you are ready to take the next step and venture into the market. This will give you some real-time experience working in a team environment and learning and sharing knowledge with others. I will suggest you brush up on the above topics again, do your part of interview preparation, talk to other folks in software testing, learn and explore new topics on automation testing and non-functional testing from other sources. If you are interested to know how testing is done in Agile projects, you can also refer to my new book, "**The Self-Taught Agile Tester**." You may also try to get certified on your testing skills through The International Software Testing Qualifications Board (ISTQB). For more details check out https://www.istqb.org/

The ultimate aim of all the above is to get you into a project as a tester be it as a freelancer, part-time or full-time role, as soon as possible. I hope this book will always guide you on your future projects and your testing career.

All the best for the new journey. May the force be with you.

33 Glossary of Terms

The following terms and their definitions have been referenced in this document.

Term	Definition
ALM	Application Lifecycle Management – Tool used for Test management
BRD	Business Requirement Document
BA	Business Analyst
BV	Business Validation or User Acceptance Test (UAT): A final validation performed by the Business to ensure a level of comfort before Implementation. Validation should mimic the business scenarios performed in an end-users' day-to-day working life.
BAU	Business as Usual; Team responsible for managing the system when it is live
DEV team	Development team
DBA	Database Administrator
Exploratory testing	An approach to testing where the testers dynamically design and execute tests based on their knowledge, exploration of the test item, and the results of previous tests.
FDD	Functional Design Document
Go live	The planned date for the system to be implemented
IMT	International Money Transfer- a system used as a project for this book
PIV/PVT	Post Implementation Verification/ Post Validation Testing. These tests are run in production environment and confirms new systems functionality is operating correctly. Tests should focus on high risk and business-critical processes.
REG Test	Regression Test: A baseline set of tests executed multiple times during a project and/or release.
SME	Subject Matter Expert
SRS	Software requirement specification
ST	System Testing
SIT	System Integration Testing
SLA	Service Level Agreement

SQL	Structured Query Language. It is used to communicate with a database. The knowlege of SQL is relevant for testers as they may have to check the data stored in database as part of testing.
SWIFT	The Society for Worldwide Interbank Financial Telecommunication (SWIFT). It is an electronic payment messaging system that enables financial institutions worldwide to send and receive information about financial transactions in a secure, standardized and reliable environment. In our project this system is used to get the latest exchange rates and once the customer confirms the International transfer a SWIFT message is sent to the destination bank via SWIFT.
SDLC	System Development Life Cycle
SRD	Scope & Requirements Document
SVP	Stress Volume Performance test
TSR	Test Summary Report
TA	Test Analyst
TL	Test Lead
Test-ware	The work products produced during the test process for use in planning, designing, executing, evaluating and reporting
Test charter	Documentation of the goal or objective for a test session for the exploratory testing.
Test basis	The body of knowledge used as the basis for test analysis and design.
TDD	Technical Design Document
UAT	User Acceptance Testing
UT	Unit Test: Confirms an individual software component operates as expected.
UFT	Unified Functional Testing: Automation tool for regression testing
UI	User Interface
Work Product	A Work Product is an artifact, deliverable, or outcome resulting from a process. Different roles may use Work Products to perform tasks and produce new Work Products in the course of performing these tasks.

Made in the USA
Monee, IL
26 October 2023

45245365R00122